QUICK AND EASY STUDENTS VEGETARIAN COOKBOOK

by
Sarah Sanderson

D1135726

foulsham
LONDON . NEW YORK . TORONTO . SYDNEY

foulsham

Bennetts Close, Cippenham, Berkshire SL1 5AP

Thanks to my family who had to eat all my experiments.
Also to Sue, Ali, Jo and everyone else who helped me.
Finally to Plymouth Claimants' Union for being ace.

ISBN 0-572-02042-2

Printed and bound in Great Britain by
Cox & Wyman Ltd, Reading, Berkshire

CONTENTS

INTRODUCTION

This is not a cookery book for vegetarians; it is a cookery book for those who really love their food but don't always want to spend lots of time preparing it. Some of the recipes take a little longer than others, but they are ones which you can prepare then pop into the oven or leave on the hob and forget until the timer pings! You want to spend all your time eating it, don't you? Me too! I was a student until earlier this year so I know what it's like to try to fill your belly on a very small amount of money. This is the food I ate (and still do) and still had enough over from my grant to go down the pub –no, sorry, I mean to buy books with.

Cooking for One?

The recipes in this book will feed three to four people unless you are particularly greedy. From personal experience, most students would not bother to 'cook' solely for themselves, but cook communally in shared houses and halls. If you are cooking for one, you can either make the full quantity and reheat some for another meal, or simply cut down the quantity of ingredients.

Where to Shop?

I assume that most people get the bulk of their food from supermarkets once or twice a week. This is fine for most things, but some items are outrageously expensive in supermarkets and it is really worth the extra effort to get them elsewhere. These are:

* Fruit and Vegetables: buy these from your local market or greengrocers. They will be much cheaper

* Herbs and Spices: the cheapest place for these I have found is in health food shops. My local one sells them in small plastic bags which are a third of the price of the supermarkets and sometimes less, and the selection is wider.

Health Food Shops

There is no great difference in price here between supermarkets and health food shops for many things, such as beans and pulses, but you may like to support your local store. If it is independently run you may get special deals if you are a regular customer, and the staff are more likely to be able to tell you how to cook and use new ingredients.

Cooking for Vegans*

The trouble with vegetarians is that some of their friends will have gone a step further and become vegans! Vegans, as you probably know, don't eat any animal produce whatsoever, including dairy foods. This can be a bit of a problem if you are feeding vegans and vegetarians at the same time. However, worry no more! Several recipes in this book are vegan (marked *). Where necessary, you may have to buy special vegan ingredients (also marked *) to substitute for ordinary dairy products, for example. These ingredients tend to be a little more expensive, so it is not necessary to use them unless you are catering for vegans.

Gadgets and Garlic Presses

Basically, you don't need any fancy gadgets to cook good meals. A few pans, some scales, knives and some sort of dish to put in the oven are all that are really necessary. A blender is handy for a few things, but not essential.

NOTES FOR COOKS

* It is important that either metric, Imperial or American measures are followed in all recipes, not a combination.

   Spoon measures:

   1 level tablespoon = 15 ml

   1 level teaspoon = 5 ml

   Spoon measurements in all recipes are level.

* When herbs are used in a recipe, the flavour of dried is stronger than fresh, so use half the quantity of dried. (Unless otherwise stated, dried herbs are used in this book.)

* Parsley, however, is probably the one herb that can not be substituted by the dried ingredient. The difference in taste of dried parsley when used in a cooked recipe is hardly noticeable, but it does not have the same flavour or appearance when used as a garnish for dishes. Either chop or leave in sprigs to add the finishing touch to starters and soups, main courses, vegetables or salads. A bunch of parsley placed in a glass of water and left in a cool place will keep fresh for about a week.

* Garlic purée is a good substitute for the fresh ingredient and a tube will keep for several weeks in the fridge once opened.

* The range in size of canned and packet produce varies enormously; so you need not be too precise when shopping for ingredients. Do not worry if a can size varies slightly as it will not have any great bearing on the quality of the finished dish.

* All recipes are for 3-4 servings.

Soaking and Cooking Beans

All beans and pulses must be soaked and boiled before it is safe to eat them, apart from lentils which do not need soaking. Many of the recipes use canned beans generally as they are easier, but they are also more expensive.

If you are going to soak your own beans, use about half the amount specified for canned beans. It sounds like a lot of effort but it is very simple if you can plan what you want to eat a day in advance. All you have to do is put the beans in a bowl of water and leave overnight or for at least 6 hours. Drain and rinse them in cold water. Put the beans into a pan of clean water, bring to the boil and boil vigorously for 10 minutes. Remove any scum from the surface of the water. Lower the heat and simmer for about an hour until soft.

TVP

TVP stands for textured vegetable protein. Many gourmet vegetarians frown upon it, but it is cheap and adds bulk to meals. It comes in mince and chunks, natural and beef flavoured, so take your pick. You can throw it into stews dry, but it tends to be rather chewy. Leave in a bowl of water, vegetable stock, beer, wine – anything really as it will absorb the liquid and take on some of the flavour for any time up to an hour before adding to the recipe.

Stock

All stock used in the recipes is made with boiling water and a vegetable stock cube. Feel free to make your own with fresh vegetables if you have the time. Simply boil up a selection of fresh vegetables in a pan of water and simmer for 20 minutes then strain. If you can be bothered to do this every time then you are a more patient person than I am – well done!

Soups

Soups always sound so dull and what you are given if you're ill – but not any more! These are delicious, most cost under £1 for three or four people, so they are amazingly cheap as well as filling. Serve them with crusty bread for a complete meal.

POTATO AND LEEK SOUP*

ingredients	Metric	Imperial	American
Margarine*	25 g	1 oz	2 tbsp
Leeks, sliced	3	3	3
Potatoes, sliced	675 g	1½ lb	1½ lb
Vegetable stock	600 ml	1 pt	2 ½ cups
Salt and pepper			
Milk* or water			

method

1. Melt the margarine in a large pan and stir in the leeks. Cook gently for 10 minutes until softened.

2. Add the potatoes and stock and a little salt and pepper. Bring to the boil then lower the heat, cover and simmer for about 30 minutes until all the ingredients are soft.

3. Remove from the heat and leave to cool for a few minutes. You can leave the soup lumpy, blend it in a blender or push it through a sieve with a spoon; the choice is yours!

4. Reheat the soup gently and stir in a little milk or water if it is too thick. Serve with crusty bread.

variation

Leeks can be replaced with 2 onions – they are usually cheaper.

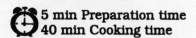 5 min Preparation time
40 min Cooking time

Noodle Soup*

ingredients	Metric	Imperial	American
Vegetable stock	1.8 l	3 pts	7½ cups
Salt			
Lemon grass, chopped	5 ml	1 tsp	1 tsp
Soy sauce	5 ml	1 tsp	1 tsp
Vermicelli	175 g	6 oz	6 oz

method

1. Bring the stock to the boil with the salt, lemon grass and soy sauce.

2. Add the vermicelli and simmer for 5 minutes until just tender. Check and adjust the seasoning if necessary.

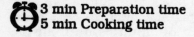
3 min Preparation time
5 min Cooking time

SPEEDY PEA SOUP*

ingredients	Metric	Imperial	American
Vegetable stock	1.2 l	2 pts	5 cups
Frozen peas, thawed	225 g	8 oz	2 cups
Chopped fresh mint	15 ml	1 tbsp	1 tbsp
Milk*	60 ml	4 tbsp	4 tbsp
Salt and pepper			

method

1. Bring the stock to the boil. Add the peas and simmer for 2-3 minutes.

2. Purée in a blender or rub through a sieve.

3. Return to the pan, add the remaining ingredients and reheat gently. Serve with crusty bread.

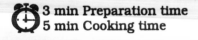
3 min Preparation time
5 min Cooking time

CHILLED TOMATO SOUP

ingredients	Metric	Imperial	American
Can chopped tomatoes	400 g	14 oz	14 oz
Red wine vinegar	15 ml	1 tbsp	1 tbsp
Olive oil	15 ml	1 tbsp	1 tbsp
Crème fraîche	45 ml	3 tbsp	3 tbsp
Mustard	2.5 ml	½ tsp	½ tsp
Dried basil	5 ml	1 tsp	1 tsp
Salt and pepper			

method

1. Rub the tomatoes through a sieve.

2. Add all the remaining ingredients and mix well.

3. Season to taste and chill before serving

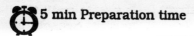 5 min Preparation time

WELSH SOUP*

ingredients	Metric	Imperial	American
Red lentils	100 g	4 oz	⅔ cup
Water	1.2 l	2 pts	5 cups
Leeks, chopped	2	2	2
Medium potatoes, chopped	4	4	4
Carrots, chopped	3	3	3
Parsnip, chopped	1	1	1
Small turnips, chopped	2	2	2
Swede, chopped	1	1	1
Vegetable stock cube	1	1	1
Salt and pepper			

method

1. Place the lentils in a pan with the water; they should be just covered. Bring to the boil then skim off any scum.

2. Add the vegetables and stock cube, return to the boil then simmer for about 20 minutes until the soup is thick and the vegetables soft. Season to taste.

note

The quantities of the ingredients are totally negotiable. The amounts given are just to give you a rough idea; put in as little or as much as you like – experiment!

5 min Preparation time
20 min Cooking time

LENTIL SOUP*

ingredients	Metric	Imperial	American
Oil	15 ml	1 tbsp	1 tbsp
Onion, chopped	1	1	1
Garlic cloves, crushed	2	2	2
Red lentils	175 g	6 oz	1 cup
Water	900 ml	1½ pts	3¾ cups
Marjoram	10 ml	2 tsp	2 tsp
Salt and pepper			

method

1. Heat the oil and fry the onion and garlic until soft. Drain off the oil.

2. Add the remaining ingredients, bring to the boil then simmer for 30 minutes. Adjust the seasoning to taste. Serve with crusty bread.

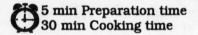 5 min Preparation time
30 min Cooking time

TOMATO SOUP*

ingredients	Metric	Imperial	American
Can chopped tomatoes	400 g	14 oz	14 oz
Milk*	300 ml	½ pt	1¼ cups
Dried oregano	5 ml	1 tsp	1 tsp
Pepper			

method

1. Blend together all the ingredients.

2. Place in a saucepan and heat through. Serve hot.

note
You will need some sort of blending device for this one.

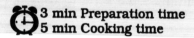

3 min Preparation time
5 min Cooking time

SWEETCORN SOUP*

ingredients	Metric	Imperial	American
Oil	5 ml	1 tsp	1 tsp
Onion, chopped	1	1	1
Potatoes, sliced	450 g	1 lb	1 lb
Can sweetcorn	350 g	12 oz	3 cups
Vegetable stock	900 ml	1½ pts	3¾ cups
Salt and pepper			

method

1. Heat the oil and fry the onion for 3 minutes.

2. Add the remaining ingredients. Bring to the boil then simmer for 30 minutes.

3. Blend, mash or leave lumpy. Reheat if necessary and serve hot.

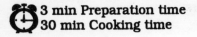 3 min Preparation time
30 min Cooking time

GARLIC SOUP*

ingredients	Metric	Imperial	American
Vegetable stock	900 ml	1½ pts	3¾ cups
Garlic cloves, crushed	4	4	4
Dried sage	5 ml	1 tsp	1 tsp
Bay leaves	3	3	3
Cloves	4	4	4
Salt and pepper			

method

1. Bring all the ingredients to the boil in a saucepan then simmer for 45 minutes. Discard the bay leaves and cloves. Serve hot with bread or toast.

note

Adjust the amount of garlic you use to your own taste.

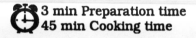

3 min Preparation time
45 min Cooking time

Carrot Soup*

ingredients	Metric	Imperial	American
Carrots, sliced	675 g	1½ lb	1½ lb
Salt			
Vegetable stock	600 ml	1 pt	2½ cups
Ground cumin	2.5 ml	½ tsp	½ tsp
Ground coriander	2.5 ml	½ tsp	½ tsp
Pepper			

method

1. Cook the carrots in boiling salted water for about 15 minutes until soft. Drain and mash.

2. Add the mashed carrots to the stock and seasonings. Bring to the boil then simmer for 10 minutes.

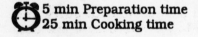
5 min Preparation time
25 min Cooking time

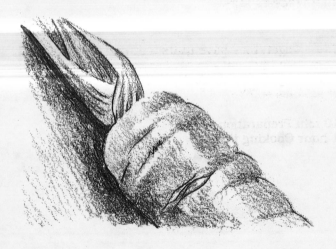

SWEDE AND CAULIFLOWER SOUP*

ingredients	Metric	Imperial	American
Cauliflower, cut into florets	1	1	1
Swede, diced	1	1	1
Onion, sliced	1	1	1
Vegetable stock	1.2 l	2 pts	5 cups
Salt and pepper			
Tomato purée (paste)	15 ml	1 tbsp	1 tbsp
Chopped fresh thyme	15 ml	1 tbsp	1 tbsp

method

1. Place the vegetables and stock in a saucepan, bring to the boil then simmer for at least 1 hour until the vegetables are soft.

2. Season with salt and pepper, tomato purée and thyme and continue to simmer over a low heat until ready to serve.

variation

These vegetables have quite a strong flavour. Add a few diced potatoes to weaken the taste, if desired. The longer you cook the soup, the softer the vegetables will be.

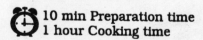 10 min Preparation time
1 hour Cooking time

MINESTRONE SOUP*

ingredients	Metric	Imperial	American
Vegetable stock	600 ml	1 pt	2 ½ cups
Tomato purée (paste)	15 ml	1 tbsp	1 tbsp
Minestrone pasta or spaghetti	75 g	3 oz	3 oz
Carrots, diced	2	2	2
Onion, chopped	1	1	1
Garlic clove, crushed	1	1	1
Frozen peas, thawed	100 g	4 oz	1 cup
Dried mixed herbs	15 ml	1 tbsp	1 tbsp

method

1. Bring all the ingredients to the boil in a saucepan then simmer for 30 minutes. Serve hot.

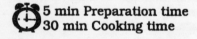 5 min Preparation time
30 min Cooking time

FRUIT SOUP*

ingredients	Metric	Imperial	American
Soft fruit such as raspberries, strawberries, blackcurrants	450 g	1 lb	1 lb
Sugar	100 g	4 oz	½ cup
Milk*	900 ml	1½ pts	3¾ cups

method

1. Heat the fruit gently until soft. Mash and whisk with the sugar. Rub through a sieve to remove any pips, if you wish.

2. Bring the milk to the boil then allow it to cool before slowly stirring into the fruit.

3. Chill before serving

⏰ 3 min Preparation time
15 min Cooking time plus chilling

MILK SOUP WITH CROÛTONS

ingredients	Metric	Imperial	American
Slice bread, cubed	1	1	1
Margarine for frying			
Milk	300 ml	½ pt	1¼ cups
Salt			
Egg, beaten	1	1	1
Curry powder	5 ml	1 tsp	1 tsp
Pepper			
Pinch of dried basil			

method

1. Fry the bread in the margarine until crisp to make the croûtons.

2. Heat the milk with a pinch of salt. Slowly add the egg and curry powder. Stir and heat until thickened, without allowing the soup to boil. Season with salt, pepper and basil.

3. Serve sprinkled with croûtons.

5 min Preparation time
15 min Cooking time

POT MEALS

These meals need no oven and don't make too much washing up.

TAGLIATELLE*

ingredients	Metric	Imperial	American
Tagliatelle	225 g	8 oz	8 oz
Salt			
Margarine*	15 ml	1 tbsp	1 tbsp
Onion, chopped	1	1	1
Garlic clove, crushed	1	1	1
Mushrooms, sliced	100 g	4 oz	¼ lb
Sweetcorn kernels	30 ml	2 tbsp	2 tbsp
Single (light) cream*	150 ml	¼ pt	⅔ cup
Pepper			
Pinch of dried mixed herbs			

method

1. Cook the pasta in boiling salted water until just tender. Drain.

2. Melt the margarine and fry the onion, garlic and mushrooms for 5 minutes until soft.

3. Stir in the pasta, sweetcorn and cream and heat through. Season to taste with salt, pepper and herbs.

4. Serve with bread and peas.

note

Cream can be substituted with crème fraîche* if you prefer.

5 min Preparation time
10 min Cooking time

CREAMY PASTA

ingredients	Metric	Imperial	American
Pasta shells	225 g	8 oz	½ lb
Salt			
Single (light) cream	300 ml	½ pt	1¼ cups
Soft cheese	100 g	4 oz	½ cup
Dried tarragon	5 ml	1 tsp	1 tsp
Pepper			

method

1. Cook the pasta in boiling salted water until tender. Drain.

2. Heat the cream, cheese and seasonings gently then stir in the pasta.

3. Serve with warm crusty bread and salad.

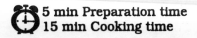
5 min Preparation time
15 min Cooking time

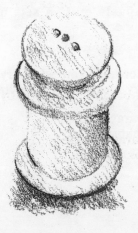

NUTTY PASTA*

ingredients	Metric	Imperial	American
Butter or margarine*	25 g	1 oz	2 tbsp
Onion, thinly sliced	1	1	1
Mushrooms, sliced	225 g	8 oz	½ lb
Walnuts, chopped	175 g	3 oz	¾ cup
Soured (dairy sour) cream*	300 ml	½ pt	1¼ cups
Pinch of dried tarragon			
Pepper			
Tagliatelle or pasta	175 g	6 oz	6 oz

method

1. Melt the butter or margarine and fry the onion and mushrooms for 4 minutes until soft.

2. Add the walnuts, cream and seasonings and heat through, stirring.

3. Meanwhile, cook the tagliatelle in boiling salted water for about 10 minutes until just tender. Drain well.

4. Spoon the pasta on to a serving plate and pour over the sauce.

note

If you do not have soured (dairy sour) cream, just use ordinary cream and add a little lemon juice.

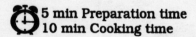 5 min Preparation time
10 min Cooking time

ROB'S SLOB CURRY*

ingredients	Metric	Imperial	American
Can thick vegetable soup	400 g	14 oz	14 oz
Frozen peas, thawed	50 g	2 oz	½ cup
Frozen sweetcorn, thawed	50 g	2 oz	½ cup
Potato, diced	1	1	1
Chilli powder	5 ml	1 tsp	1 tsp
Hot curry powder	5 ml	1 tsp	1 tsp
Milk*	60 ml	4 tbsp	4 tbsp

method

1. Bring all the ingredients except the milk to the boil in a saucepan then simmer for 15 minutes until the potato is tender.

2. Add the milk and cook for 5 minutes.

3. Serve with rice and Indian bread.

note

This one comes from my 14-year-old nephew whose stomach knows no limits.

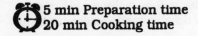
5 min Preparation time
20 min Cooking time

VEGETABLE CURRY*

ingredients	Metric	Imperial	American
Oil	30 ml	2 tbsp	2 tbsp
Bay leaves	2	2	2
Cinnamon stick	2.5 cm	1 in	1 in
Cardamom pods	10	10	10
Cloves	5	5	5
Ground coriander	15 ml	1 tbsp	1 tbsp
Ground cumin	15 ml	1 tbsp	1 tbsp
Pinch of chilli powder			
Sweet pickle	10 ml	2 tsp	2 tsp
Tomato purée (paste)	15 ml	1 tbsp	1 tbsp
Garlic cloves	2	2	2
Onion, chopped	1	1	1
Potatoes, diced	450 g	1 lb	1 lb
Frozen peas, thawed	100 g	4 oz	1 cup
Vegetable stock	150 ml	¼ pt	⅔ cup
Salt and pepper			
Creamed coconut	50-75 g	2-3 oz	2-3 oz
Garam masala	15 ml	1 tbsp	1 tbsp

method

1. Heat the oil and fry the spices, pickle and tomato purée for 1 minute. Add the garlic and onion and fry for 3 minutes.

2. Add the vegetables and stock, bring to the boil then simmer for at least 1 hour, adding more water if the mixture becomes too dry.

3. Stir in the coconut and garam masala just before serving and heat through.

4. Serve with rice, raita and popadums.

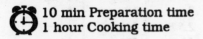

variations

This can be made with any vegetables or with TVP. It tastes much better with a selection of spices rather than with just curry powder and you can change the quantities of the spices as you become more adventurous.

10 min Preparation time
1 hour Cooking time

CURRIED EGGS

ingredients	Metric	Imperial	American
Margarine	25 g	1 oz	2 tbsp
Onion, chopped	1	1	1
Plain (all-purpose) flour	15 ml	1 tbsp	1 tbsp
Curry powder	15 ml	1 tbsp	1 tbsp
Vegetable stock	600 ml	1 pt	2½ cups
Sweet pickle	5 ml	1 tsp	1 tsp
Creamed coconut	25 g	1 oz	1 oz
Hard-boiled (hard-cooked) eggs, halved	4	4	4
Dash of lemon juice			
Salt and pepper			

method

1. Melt the margarine and fry the onion for a few minutes until soft.

2. Add the flour and curry powder and cook, stirring, for 1-2 minutes.

3. Add the stock and stir until smooth. Simmer for 20 minutes.

4. Add the remaining ingredients and simmer for a further 3-4 minutes.

5. Serve with rice and other spicy dishes.

10 min Preparation time
30 min Cooking time

EASY VEGETABLE CURRY*

ingredients	Metric	Imperial	American
Swede, diced	1	1	1
Curry powder	5 ml	1 tsp	1 tsp
Pepper			
Tomato purée (paste)	10 ml	2 tsp	2 tsp
Frozen mixed vegetables, thawed	450 g	1 lb	1 lb
Eating (dessert) apple, peeled and diced	1	1	1

method

1. Cook the swede in a little water with the curry powder, pepper and tomato purée for about 15 minutes until tender.

2. Stir in the vegetables and apple, bring to the boil then simmer for 10 minutes.

3. Serve with rice.

note

This is not at all authentic as a curry, but it is cheap, easy and tasty.

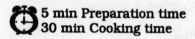
5 min Preparation time
30 min Cooking time

VEGETABLE STIR-FRY*

ingredients	Metric	Imperial	American
Aubergine, diced	1	1	1
Salt			
Oil	30 ml	2 tbsp	2 tbsp
Onion, chopped	1	1	1
Garlic cloves, crushed	2	2	2
Ground cloves	1.5 ml	1/4 tsp	1/4 tsp
Pinch of dried basil			
Ground ginger	2.5 ml	1/2 tsp	1/2 tsp
Courgettes, sliced	2	2	2
Yellow (bell) pepper, sliced	1	1	1
Carrots, sliced lengthways	2	2	2
Sweetcorn	50 g	2 oz	1/2 cup
Mushrooms, sliced	50 g	2 oz	2 oz
Tomato purée (paste)	15 ml	1 tbsp	1 tbsp
Soy sauce	30 ml	2 tbsp	2 tbsp
Water			
Rice:			
Long-grain rice	225 g	8 oz	1 cup
Salt			
Garlic cloves, crushed	2	2	2
Dried thyme	2.5 ml	1/2 tsp	1/2 tsp

method

1. Sprinkle the aubergine with salt and leave to drain in a colander for 20 minutes to remove the bitterness. Rinse and drain.

2. Heat the oil and fry the onion and garlic for 3 minutes. Add the aubergine, spices, courgettes, pepper and carrots and stir well. Add the sweetcorn and mushrooms.

3. Stir in the tomato purée and soy sauce. Add just enough water to make a sauce and simmer for about 15 minutes until the vegetables are just soft.

4. Meanwhile cook the rice in boiling water with the garlic and thyme for the time directed on the packet. Drain well and serve with the stir-fry.

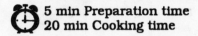 5 min Preparation time
20 min Cooking time

SWEET AND SOUR STIR-FRY*

ingredients	Metric	Imperial	American
Oil	15 ml	1 tbsp	1 tbsp
Onion, sliced	1	1	1
Red or green (bell) pepper, sliced	1	1	1
Mushrooms, sliced	175 g	6 oz	6 oz
Canned pineapple chunks in juice	450 g	1 lb	1 lb
Tomato ketchup (catsup)	30 ml	2 tbsp	2 tbsp
Soy sauce	30 ml	2 tbsp	2 tbsp
Vinegar	30 ml	2 tbsp	2 tbsp
Honey	15 ml	1 tbsp	1 tbsp
Vegetable stock	60 ml	4 tbsp	4 tbsp
Cornflour (cornstarch)	15 ml	1 tbsp	1 tbsp
Pepper			
Beansprouts	225 g	6 oz	6 oz

method

1. Heat the oil in a wok or large frying pan (skillet) until almost smoking. Add the onion, pepper and mushrooms and stir-fry for 3-4 minutes.

2. Meanwhile, mix together all the remaining ingredients except the beansprouts. Add to the pan and heat through, stirring.

3. Add the beansprouts and stir-fry for 2 minutes until hot.

4. Serve at once with rice or noodles.

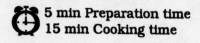
5 min Preparation time
15 min Cooking time

SQUASHED KIDNEY BEANS*

ingredients	Metric	Imperial	American
Oil	30 ml	2 tbsp	2 tbsp
Onion, chopped	1	1	1
Garlic cloves, crushed	2	2	2
Chilli powder	5 ml	1 tsp	1 tsp
Salt	5 ml	1 tsp	1 tsp
Tomato ketchup (catsup)	60 ml	4 tbsp	4 tbsp
Kidney beans, soaked and cooked (page 6)	225 g	8 oz	1⅔ cups
Cheese, grated*	175 g	6 oz	1½ cups

method

1. Heat the oil in a large frying pan (skillet) or wok and fry the onion and garlic for about 4 minutes until soft.

2. Stir in the chilli powder, salt and ketchup.

3. Drain the beans, reserving the water. Mash the beans with a fork or potato masher. Add them to the pan with a little of the reserved water until the mixture is thick and moist but not too runny. Stir until heated through.

4. Stir in the cheese until melted.

5. Serve with rice, bread and salad.

note
Use leftovers for Kidney Bean Pâté (page 115).

5 min Preparation time
15 min Cooking time

MUSHROOM STROGANOFF*

ingredients	Metric	Imperial	American
Butter or margarine*	75 g	3 oz	⅓ cup
Onion, chopped	1	1	1
Garlic cloves, crushed	2	2	2
Mushrooms, sliced	1.6 kg	3½ lb	3½ lb
White wine	150 ml	¼ pt	⅔ cup
Cornflour (cornstarch)	15 ml	1 tbsp	1 tbsp
Single (light) cream*	300 ml	½ pt	1¼ cups
Lemon juice	15 ml	1 tbsp	1 tbsp
Salt and pepper			

method

1. Melt the butter or margarine and fry the onion and garlic for a few minutes until softened.

2. Add the mushrooms and simmer for up to 30 minutes until the liquid has evaporated.

3. Add the wine and simmer for 5 minutes.

4. Mix the cornflour with a little water then stir it into the pan with the cream. Bring to the boil then simmer for 5 minutes until thickened, stirring continuously.

5. Add the lemon juice and seasoning.

6. Serve hot with rice and pasta.

note

This is a little extravagant but tastes beautiful. You will need this huge amount of mushrooms as it reduces down a lot.

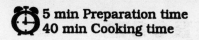
CASHEW PAELLA*

ingredients	Metric	Imperial	American
Oil	15 ml	1 tbsp	1 tbsp
Leek, chopped	1	1	1
Red (bell) pepper, chopped	1	1	1
Green (bell) pepper, chopped	1	1	1
Mushrooms, sliced	100 g	4 oz	1/4 lb
Long-grain rice	225 g	8 oz	1 cup
Cashew nuts	100 g	4 oz	1 cup
Vegetable stock	600 ml	1 pt	2 1/2 cups
Pepper			
Pinch of dried mixed herbs			

method

1. Heat the oil and fry the vegetables gently for 5 minutes until soft.

2. Add the rice and fry for a further 3 minutes, stirring.

3. Add the nuts, stock and seasoning, bring to the boil and simmer for about 30 minutes until the rice is cooked and most of the water has been absorbed, stirring occasionally.

4. Serve hot with salad.

8 min Preparation time
40 min Cooking time

SUE'S STEW*

ingredients	Metric	Imperial	American
Oil	15 ml	1 tbsp	1 tbsp
Large onion, chopped	1	1	1
Red (bell) pepper, sliced	1	1	1
Garlic clove, crushed	1	1	1
Ground cumin	5 ml	1 tsp	1 tsp
Ground coriander	5 ml	1 tsp	1 tsp
Cinnamon	1.5 ml	¼ tsp	¼ tsp
Ground cloves	1.5 ml	¼ tsp	¼ tsp
Pinch of chilli powder			
Tomato purée (paste)	15 ml	1 tbsp	1 tbsp
Vegetable stock cube	1	1	1
Chick peas, soaked and boiled for 15 mins (page 6)	100 g	4 oz	⅔ cup
Haricot or pinto beans, soaked and boiled for 15 mins (page 6)	100 g	4 oz	⅔ cup
Black eye or kidney beans, soaked and boiled for 15 mins (page 6)	100 g	4 oz	⅔ cup
Dried mixed herbs	5 ml	1 tsp	1 tsp

method

1. Heat the oil and fry the onion, pepper, garlic and spices for 5 minutes, stirring.

2. Add the tomato purée, stock cube, beans and herbs, bring to the boil then cover and simmer for about 1 hour until the beans are soft. Check occasionally and add a little water if the mixture becomes too dry.

3. Serve with pitta or naan bread.

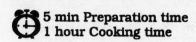

variation

Use a choice of beans from what you have in store.

⏰ 5 min Preparation time
1 hour Cooking time

SPICY PINTO STEW*

ingredients	Metric	Imperial	American
Oil	15 ml	1 tbsp	1 tbsp
Garlic clove, crushed	1	1	1
Ginger	2.5 ml	½ tsp	½ tsp
Pinto beans, soaked and boiled (page 6)	175 g	6 oz	1 cup
Can chopped tomatoes	200 g	7 oz	7 oz
Onion, chopped	1	1	1
Soy sauce	30 ml	2 tbsp	2 tbsp
Five spice powder	5 ml	1 tsp	1 tsp
Vegetable stock	150 ml	¼ pt	⅔ cup
Red (bell) pepper, chopped	1	1	1
Mushrooms, sliced	225 g	8 oz	½ lb
Courgettes, sliced	4	4	4
Salt and pepper			

method

1. Heat the oil and fry the garlic and ginger very gently for 2 minutes.

2. Add the beans and the remaining ingredients, bring to the boil, cover and simmer for 20 minutes.

3. Season to taste then serve hot with bread or rice.

⏰ 5 min Preparation time
30 min Cooking time

ANTOINE'S BEAN STEW*

ingredients

ingredients	Metric	Imperial	American
Oil	5 ml	1 tsp	1 tsp
Onion, chopped	1	1	1
Can baked beans	400 g	14 oz	14 oz
Can chopped tomatoes	400 g	14 oz	14 oz
Can kidney beans in chilli sauce	400 g	14 oz	14 oz

method

1. Heat the oil and fry the onion for 3 minutes until soft.

2. Add the remaining ingredients and heat through, stirring. Serve at once!

note

This was created by Anthony, who trained as a chef, but hates cooking himself!

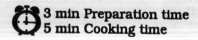

3 min Preparation time
5 min Cooking time

TASTY CHILLI*

ingredients	Metric	Imperial	American
Oil	15 ml	1 tbsp	1 tbsp
Garlic cloves, crushed	2	2	2
Onion, chopped	1	1	1
Chilli powder	5 ml	1 tsp	1 tsp
TVP mince	100 g	4 oz	¼ lb
Can tomatoes	400 g	14 oz	14 oz
Tomato purée (paste)	30 ml	2 tbsp	2 tbsp
Mushrooms, sliced	100 g	4 oz	¼ lb
Can kidney beans	400 g	14 oz	14 oz
Vegetable stock cube	1	1	1
Yeast extract	15 ml	1 tbsp	1 tbsp
Salt and pepper			

method

1. Heat the oil and fry the garlic, onion and chilli powder for 3 minutes until soft.

2. Add the remaining ingredients with any leftover wine. Bring to the boil and simmer for at least 45 minutes, adding a little water if the mixture becomes too dry. Adjust the seasoning to taste.

3. Serve with rice and bread or jacket potatoes.

variations

This tastes even better if left and reheated the next day. Any leftovers can be topped with mashed potatoes to make a cottage pie.

note

Chilli powders vary in strength, so use an amount to suit your taste.

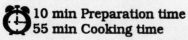 10 min Preparation time
55 min Cooking time

41

SPAGHETTI BOLOGNESE*

ingredients	Metric	Imperial	American
TVP mince	175 g	6 oz	6 oz
Oil	15 ml	1 tbsp	1 tbsp
Onion, chopped	1	1	1
Garlic clove, crushed	1	1	1
Mushrooms	100 g	4 oz	¼ lb
Can tomatoes	400 g	14 oz	14 oz
Tomato purée (paste)	30 ml	2 tbsp	2 tbsp
Red wine	120 ml	4 fl oz	½ cup
Yeast extract	15 ml	1 tbsp	1 tbsp
Vinegar	2.5 ml	½ tsp	½ tsp
Sugar	2.5 ml	½ tsp	½ tsp
Dried mixed herbs	5 ml	1 tsp	1 tsp
Salt and pepper			
Spaghetti	225 g	8 oz	½ lb

method

1. Soak the TVP for 15 minutes in boiling water. Drain.

2. Heat the oil and fry the onion and garlic until soft. Add the remaining ingredients expect the spaghetti and simmer for 30 minutes.

3. Meanwhile, cook the spaghetti in boiling salted water until just tender. Drain.

4. Spoon the spaghetti on to a serving dish and pour the sauce over the top.

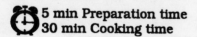 5 min Preparation time
30 min Cooking time

CREAMY STROGANOFF*

ingredients	Metric	Imperial	American
TVP chunks	175 g	6 oz	6 oz
Red wine or stock for soaking			
Margarine*	25 g	1 oz	2 tbsp
Onions, chopped	2	2	2
Garlic cloves, crushed	4	4	4
Dried mixed herbs	5 ml	1 tsp	1 tsp
Mushrooms, sliced	100 g	4 oz	¼ lb
Red wine	120 ml	4 fl oz	½ cup
White Sauce* (page 112)	300 ml	½ pt	1¼ cups
Dried tarragon	5 ml	1 tsp	1 tsp
Salt and pepper			

method

1   Soak the TVP in wine or stock for 1 hour. Drain.

2.   Melt the margarine and fry the onions, garlic and herbs for 3 minutes. Add the TVP, mushrooms and wine and simmer for 5 minutes.

3.   Add the white sauce, tarragon and salt and pepper. Simmer for 20 minutes until the TVP is tender. Serve with pasta.

5 min Preparation time
30 min Cooking time

SWEDISH TVP

ingredients	Metric	Imperial	American
Onion, thinly sliced	1	1	1
Mushrooms, quartered	100 g	4 oz	¼ lb
TVP chunks, soaked in	100 g	4 oz	¼ lb
stock	300 ml	½ pt	1¼ cups
Soy sauce	2.5 ml	½ tsp	½ tsp
Yeast extract	7.5 ml	1½ tsp	1½ tsp
Dried basil	2.5 ml	½ tsp	½ tsp
Vegetable stock	150 ml	¼ pt	⅔ cup
Plain (all-purpose) flour	15 ml	1 tbsp	1 tbsp
Quark	100 g	4 oz	½ cup

method

1. Put the onion, mushrooms, TVP and soaking stock into a large pan and bring to the boil. Add the seasonings, cover and simmer for about 1 hour.

2. Mix together the stock, flour and quark to a thick paste and stir into the stew. Heat through, stirring.

3. Serve with pasta.

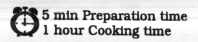
5 min Preparation time
1 hour Cooking time

TVP MATTAR

ingredients	Metric	Imperial	American
Oil	15 ml	1 tbsp	1 tbsp
Onions, chopped	2	2	2
Cloves garlic, crushed	3	3	3
Frozen peas, thawed	350 g	12 oz	3 cups
Ground ginger	5 ml	1 tsp	1 tsp
Chilli powder	5 ml	1 tsp	1 tsp
Ground cumin	10 ml	2 tsp	2 tsp
Ground coriander	15 ml	1 tbsp	1 tbsp
Chopped fresh mint	30 ml	2 tbsp	2 tbsp
Salt	2.5 ml	½ tsp	½ tsp
TVP mince, soaked in stock	225 g	8 oz	½ lb
Yeast extract	10 ml	2 tsp	2 tsp
Natural (plain) yoghurt	150 ml	¼ pt	⅔ cup
Lemon juice	45 ml	3 tbsp	3 tbsp

method

1. Heat the oil and fry the vegetables, spices and salt for a few minutes until softened.

2. Add the TVP and yeast extract, bring to the boil, cover and simmer for 30 minutes.

3. Stir in the yoghurt and lemon juice and stir until absorbed and heated through.

4. Serve hot with rice and chapatis.

variation

This is really beefy and rich for any of you out there with meat cravings! You can use cream cheese or quark instead of yoghurt , but cheese is not quite as healthy.

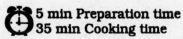 5 min Preparation time
35 min Cooking time

45

FRENCH OMELETTE

These are ingredients per person.

ingredients	Metric	Imperial	American
Eggs	2	2	2
Dried marjoram	1.5 ml	¼ tsp	¼ tsp
Milk	15 ml	1 tbsp	1 tbsp
Salt and pepper			
Oil for frying			
Onion, chopped	½	½	½
Brie or Camembert	50 g	2 oz	2 oz

method

1. Beat together the eggs, herbs, milk and seasonings.

2. Heat a little oil and lightly fry the onion for 2 minutes. Put to one side.

3. Pour the egg mixture into the pan and cook gently until almost set and firm underneath.

4. Sprinkle the onion and cheese over one half of the omelette, fold in half and press lightly. Cook for a further 1-2 minutes.

5. Serve with salad and French bread and wine.

⏰ 5 min Preparation time
10 min Cooking time

SPANISH OMELETTE

ingredients	Metric	Imperial	American
Oil	15 ml	1 tbsp	1 tbsp
Cooked potatoes, diced	225 g	8 oz	½ lb
Frozen peas, thawed	175 g	6 oz	1½ cups
Red (bell) pepper, diced	½	½	½
Mushrooms, sliced	225 g	8 oz	½ lb
Margarine	25 g	1 oz	2 tbsp
Eggs	6	6	6
Water	30 ml	2 tbsp	2 tbsp
Dried mixed herbs	15 ml	1 tbsp	1 tbsp
Salt and pepper			
Cheddar cheese, grated	175 g	6 oz	1½ cups

method

1. Heat the oil and fry the vegetables for a few minutes until soft. Add the margarine.

2. Whisk together the eggs, water and herbs and season with salt and pepper. Add to the pan and keep stirring with a fork to prevent sticking, especially in the middle.

3. When almost set, level the top and sprinkle with cheese. Brown under a hot grill (broiler) for a few minutes.

5 min Preparation time
10 min Cooking time

BASIC PANCAKE MIX

ingredients	Metric	Imperial	American
Plain (all-purpose) flour	100 g	4 oz	1 cup
Pinch of salt			
Milk	300 ml	½ pt	1¼ cups
Egg, beaten	1	1	1
Margarine	15 ml	1 tbsp	1 tbsp
Margarine for frying			

method

1. Whisk the flour, salt, milk and egg to a smooth batter. Melt the margarine then add it to the mixture.

2. Melt a knob of margarine in a frying pan (skillet). Pour in just enough mixture to cover the bottom of the pan and cook until just brown underneath. Toss or turn over and cook the otherside.

3. Serve as a sweet with sugar or lemon juice, or a savoury course filled with cottage cheese, cooked vegetables or ratatouille.

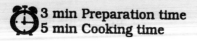

3 min Preparation time
5 min Cooking time

OVEN MEALS

It is often easy to prepare a meal and just pop it to cook in the oven. If you have an automatic timer on your oven, you can make use of this to fit cooking into your busy schedule or stop you burning your dinner when you are down the pub.

COTTAGE PIE*

ingredients	Metric	Imperial	American
TVP mince	100 g	4 oz	¼ lb
Oil	10 ml	2 tsp	2 tsp
Onion, chopped	½	½	½
Gravy	150 ml	¼ pt	⅔ cup
Tomato purée (paste)	15 ml	1 tbsp	1 tbsp
Cooked vegetables (optional)	225 g	8 oz	½ lb
Yeast extract	15 ml	1 tbsp	1 tbsp
Boiled and mashed potatoes	450 g	1 lb	1 lb

method

1. Soak the TVP in boiling water for 10 minutes. Drain.

2. Heat the oil and fry the onion for a few minutes until soft. Stir in the remaining ingredients except the potatoes and spoon into an ovenproof dish. Spread the mashed potatoes on the top.

3. Bake in a preheated oven at 200°C/400°F/gas mark 6 for 30 minutes until crisp and browned.

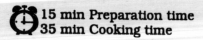 15 min Preparation time
35 min Cooking time

EGG AND MUSHROOM PIE

ingredients	Metric	Imperial	American
Potatoes	900 g	2 lb	2 lb
Butter or margarine	15 ml	1 tbsp	1 tbsp
Milk	30 ml	2 tbsp	2 tbsp
Can condensed mushroom soup	200 g	7 oz	7 oz
Hard-boiled (hard-cooked) eggs, sliced	4	4	4
Mushrooms, chopped	100 g	4 oz	¼ lb
Cheddar cheese, grated	50 g	2 oz	½ cup
Salt and pepper			

method

1. Boil the potatoes until tender then drain and mash with the butter or margarine and milk.

2. Heat the soup without allowing it to boil. Stir in the eggs and mushrooms and pour into a casserole dish. Cover with the mashed potatoes and sprinkle over the grated cheese.

3. Bake in a preheated oven at 200°C/400°F/gas mark 6 for about 15 minutes until the dish is hot and the cheese is browned.

4. Serve with green vegetables.

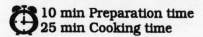

10 min Preparation time
25 min Cooking time

QUICK BEAN BAKE*

ingredients	Metric	Imperial	American
Can ratatouille	400 g	14 oz	14 oz
Can kidney beans	200 g	7 oz	7 oz
Dried tarragon	2.5 ml	½ tsp	½ tsp
Pepper			
Toasted breadcrumbs	50 g	2 oz	½ cup
Cheddar cheese*, grated	50 g	2 oz	½ cup

method

1. Heat together the ratatouille, kidney beans, tarragon and pepper then place in an ovenproof dish.

2. Mix together the breadcrumbs and cheese and sprinkle over the top. Place under the grill (broiler) or bake in a preheated oven at 200°C/400°F/gas mark 6 until the cheese has melted and browned.

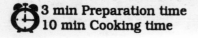

3 min Preparation time
10 min Cooking time

VEGETABLE LASAGNE*

ingredients	Metric	Imperial	American
Can ratatouille	400 g	14 oz	14 oz
Mushrooms, sliced	100 g	4 oz	¼ lb
Dried mixed herbs	5 ml	1 tsp	1 tsp
Lasagne sheets	6	6	6
Hard cheese*, grated	175 g	6 oz	1½ cups
White Sauce* (page 112)	300 ml	½ pt	1¼ cups

method

1. Mix together the ratatouille, mushrooms and herbs. Layer the mixture with the lasagne sheets in a shallow ovenproof dish.

2. Stir most of the cheese into the white sauce and pour over the top. Sprinkle with the remaining cheese. Bake in a preheated oven at 200°C/ 400°F/gas mark 6 for 30 minutes.

3. Serve with peas.

note

Some lasagne sheets need precooking, others simply need to be rinsed under hot water before assembling the dish. Check the instructions on the packet.

5 min Preparation time
35 min Cooking time

BAKED BEAN LASAGNE*

ingredients	Metric	Imperial	American
Oil	15 ml	1 tbsp	1 tbsp
Onion, chopped	1	1	1
Garlic cloves, crushed	2	2	2
Mushrooms, sliced	225 g	8 oz	½ lb
Can baked beans	400 g	14 oz	14 oz
Tomato ketchup (catsup)	30 ml	2 tbsp	2 tbsp
Soy sauce	45 ml	3 tbsp	3 tbsp
Pinch of chilli powder			
Pepper			
Lasagne sheets	8	8	8
White Sauce* (page 112)	300 ml	½ pt	1¼ cups
Cheddar cheese*, grated	175 g	6 oz	1½ cups
Parmesan cheese*, grated (optional)			

method

1. Heat the oil in a large pan and fry the onion and garlic for about 4 minutes until softened. Add the mushrooms and cook for 2 minutes.

2. Stir in the beans, tomato ketchup, soy sauce, chilli powder and pepper.

3. Layer the bean mixture and lasagne sheets in shallow ovenproof dish, finishing with a layer of lasagne. Stir the Cheddar cheese into the white sauce and pour over the top. Sprinkle with Parmesan, if using.

4. Bake in a preheated oven at 190°F/375°F/gas mark 5 for 40 minutes.

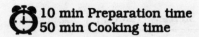

note

Some lasagne sheets need precooking, others simply need to be rinsed under hot water before assembling the dish. Check the instructions on the packet.

10 min Preparation time
50 min Cooking time

BAKED BEAN LOAF

ingredients	Metric	Imperial	American
Can baked beans	400 g	14 oz	14 oz
Small onion, chopped	1	1	1
Breadcrumbs	50 g	2 oz	½ cup
Tomato ketchup (catsup)	30 ml	2 tbsp	2 tbsp
Egg	1	1	1
Yeast extract	5 ml	1 tsp	1 tsp
Dried mixed herbs	5 ml	1 tsp	1 tsp
Salt and pepper			

method

1. Mix together all the ingredients. Pour into a greased and lined loaf tin.

2. Bake in a preheated oven at 180°C/350°F/gas mark 4 for 20 minutes.

5 min Preparation time
20 min Cooking time

ONION AND APPLE GRATIN*

ingredients	Metric	Imperial	American
Eating (dessert) apples	3-4	3-4	3-4
Onion, sliced	2	2	2
Dried sage	5 ml	1 tsp	1 tsp
Pinch of grated nutmeg			
Salt and pepper			
Crumble:			
Plain (all-purpose) flour	50 g	2 oz	½ cup
Margarine*	50 g	2 oz	¼ cup
Breadcrumbs	50 g	2 oz	½ cup

method

1. Grease an ovenproof dish. Arrange alternating layers of apple and onion in the dish, seasoning with sage, nutmeg, salt and pepper as you go.

2. Rub the flour and margarine together until the mixture resembles breadcrumbs. Stir in the breadcrumbs and sprinkle over the dish.

3. Bake in a preheated oven at 200°C/400°F/gas mark 6 for about 30 minutes until the filling is soft and the topping is golden.

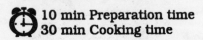
10 min Preparation time
30 min Cooking time

LENTIL PUD*

ingredients	Metric	Imperial	American
Lentils, soaked overnight	175 g	6 oz	1 cup
Garlic clove, crushed	1	1	1
Cheddar cheese*, grated	175 g	6 oz	1½ cups
Tomato ketchup (catsup)	15 ml	1 tbsp	1 tbsp
Sweet pickle	10 ml	2 tsp	2 tsp
Dash of soy sauce			
Salt and pepper			

method

1. Drain the lentils, place in a pan with fresh water, bring to the boil then simmer for about 45 minutes until tender. Drain.

2. Add the garlic, most of the cheese, the ketchup, pickle, soy sauce and salt and pepper. Pour into a greased ovenproof dish and sprinkle with the remaining cheese.

3. Bake in a preheated oven at 200°C/400°F/gas mark 6 for 20 minutes until golden.

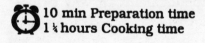 10 min Preparation time
1 ¼ hours Cooking time

DOLMAS*

ingredients	Metric	Imperial	American
Large cabbage leaves	12	12	12
Salt			
Burger mix or cooked vegetables	350 g	12 oz	12 oz
Spicy Tomato Sauce (page 110)			

method

1. Cook the leaves in boiling salted water for about 5 minutes until just soft. Drain.

2. Place a spoonful or two of burger mix on each leaf at one end and roll over to make a parcel, turning in the edges as you go. Arrange in a single layer in an ovenproof dish.

3. Bake in a preheated oven at 180°C/350°F/gas mark 4 for 15 minutes until heated through.

note

This is a good recipe for using up any leftover burger mix or vegetables.

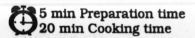
5 min Preparation time
20 min Cooking time

VEGETABLE CRUMBLE*

ingredients	Metric	Imperial	American
Courgettes, sliced	450 g	1 lb	1 lb
Salt			
Oil	15 ml	1 tbsp	1 tbsp
Red (bell) pepper, sliced	1	1	1
Mushrooms, sliced	100 g	4 oz	¼ lb
Can tomatoes	200 g	7 oz	7 oz
Garlic cloves, crushed	2	2	2
Onion, chopped	1	1	1
Pepper			
Dried marjoram	5 ml	1 tsp	1 tsp
Crumble:			
Hard cheese*, grated	175 g	6 oz	1½ cups
Breadcrumbs	100 g	4 oz	1 cup

method

1. Cook the courgettes in boiling salted water for 5 minutes. Drain.

2. Heat the oil and fry the remaining vegetables and seasoning for about 10 minutes until softened. Stir in the courgettes.

3. Spoon the vegetables into a shallow ovenproof dish. Mix together the cheese and breadcrumbs and sprinkle over the top. Bake in a preheated oven at 200°C/400°F/gas mark 6 for about 25 minutes until heated through and lightly browned.

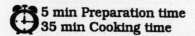 5 min Preparation time
35 min Cooking time

SPUD AND SWEDE PIE*

ingredients	Metric	Imperial	American
Potatoes, sliced	450 g	1 lb	1 lb
Swede, sliced	450 g	1 lb	1 lb
Salt			
Milk*	45 ml	3 tbsp	3 tbsp
Pepper			
Mature Cheddar cheese*, grated			
Salted crisps, lightly crushed	60 g	2 1/2 oz	2 1/2 oz

method

1. Cook the vegetables in boiling salted water for about 15 minutes until soft. Drain well then mash together. Stir in the milk and pepper. Spoon into an ovenproof dish.

2. Mix together the cheese and crisps and sprinkle over the top. Bake in a preheated oven at 200°C/400°F/gas mark 6 for 15 minutes until crisp.

3. Serve with baked beans.

⏰ 10 min Preparation time
30 min Cooking time

OVEN OMELETTE

ingredients	Metric	Imperial	American
Eggs, beaten	4	4	4
Cottage cheese	250 g	9 oz	9 oz
Milk	150 ml	¼ pt	⅔ cup
Salt and pepper			
Mushrooms, sliced	100 g	4 oz	¼ lb
Onion, chopped	1	1	1
Pinch of dried mixed herbs			

method

1. Mix all the ingredients in a bowl. Pour into a well greased ovenproof dish.

2. Bake in a preheated oven at 200°C/400°F/gas mark 6 for 20 minutes until browned and firm.

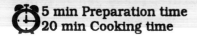 5 min Preparation time
20 min Cooking time

NUT ROAST*

ingredients	Metric	Imperial	American
Chopped mixed nuts	150 g	5 oz	1¼ cups
Breadcrumbs	75 g	3 oz	¾ cup
Onion, chopped	½	½	½
Soy sauce	15 ml	1 tbsp	1 tbsp
Dried thyme	2.5 ml	½ tsp	½ tsp
Lemon juice	5 ml	1 tsp	1 tsp
Margarine*	25 g	1 oz	2 tbsp
Oil	5 ml	1 tsp	1 tsp
Yeast extract	5 ml	1 tsp	1 tsp
Water	150 ml	¼ pt	⅔ cup

method

1. Mix all the ingredients together in a bowl, dissolving the yeast extract in the water before adding it to the mixture. Press gently into a greased loaf tin.

2. Bake in a preheated oven at 190°C/375°F/gas mark 5 for 30-40 minutes until crisp on top and hot in the centre.

3. Serve instead of meat with roast potatoes and vegetables.

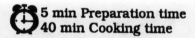
5 min Preparation time
40 min Cooking time

STUFFED PEPPERS*

ingredients	Metric	Imperial	American
Red or green (bell) peppers	4	4	4
Packet savoury rice, any flavour	1	1	1
Oil			

method

1. Remove the stem, core and seeds of the peppers.

2. Cook the rice as directed on the packet. Stuff the rice into the peppers and add a drop of oil to each one.

3. Bake in a preheated oven at 200°C/400°F/gas mark 6 for 20 minutes until tender.

note

You can, of course, make your own stuffing mixture, but why bother?

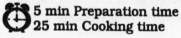

5 min Preparation time
25 min Cooking time

CHEESE AND CHIVE PANCAKES

ingredients	Metric	Imperial	American
Quantity Pancake Mix			
(page 48)	*1*	*1*	*1*
Cottage cheese	*225 g*	*8 oz*	*½ cup*
Chopped fresh chives	*15 ml*	*1 tbsp*	*1 tbsp*
Salt and pepper			
Butter or margarine	*15 ml*	*1 tbsp*	*1 tbsp*

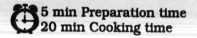

method

1. Make the pancakes as directed on page 48.

2. Mix together the cheese and chives and season with salt and pepper. Place a few spoonfuls on each pancake and roll them up. Arrange them in shallow ovenproof dish. Dot with butter or margarine.

3. Bake in a preheated oven at 200°C/400°F/gas mark 6 for about 15 minutes until heated through.

5 min Preparation time
20 min Cooking time

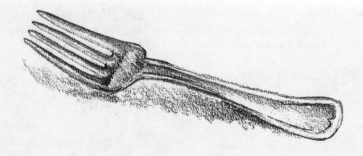

SPINACH AND RICOTTA PANCAKES

ingredients	Metric	Imperial	American
Quantity Pancake Mix			
(page 48)	1	1	1
Ricotta cheese	225 g	8 oz	½ lb
Frozen spinach, thawed	75 g	3 oz	3 oz
Salt and pepper			
Butter or margarine	15 ml	1 tbsp	1 tbsp

method

1. Make the pancakes as directed on page 48.

2. Mix together the cheese, spinach, salt and pepper. Place a few spoonfuls on each pancake and roll them up. Arrange them in a shallow ovenproof dish. Dot with butter or margarine.

3. Bake in a preheated oven at 200°C/400°F/gas mark 6 for about 15 minutes until heated through.

variations

If you use fresh spinach, you will need to cook it for a few minutes then drain it well.

You can also fill pancakes with Squashed Kidney Beans (page 35), canned ratatouille, canned chopped tomatoes with herbs or many other variations.

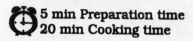 5 min Preparation time
20 min Cooking time

CHEATY VEGETABLE PIE*

ingredients	Metric	Imperial	American
Pastry:			
Plain (all-purpose) flour	225 g	8 oz	2 cups
Pinch of salt			
Margarine*	100 g	4 oz	½ cup
Water	60 ml	4 tbsp	4 tbsp
Filling:			
Mixed vegetables	175 g	6 oz	6 oz
Canned mushroom soup	400 g	14 oz	14 oz
Dried mixed herbs	5 ml	1 tsp	1 tsp
Milk			

method

1. Mix together the flour and salt. Rub in the margarine until the mixture resembles breadcrumbs. Stir in the water a little at a time until the mixture comes together in a dough. Gently mould the dough in floured hands until smooth.

2. Roll out two-thirds of the dough and use to line a 20 cm/8 in pie dish.

3. Heat the vegetables in a pan of water for a few minutes then drain. Mix with the soup and herbs and pour into the pastry mould.

4. Roll out the remaining pastry and lay over the top, sealing the edges together with a little water. Brush the top with milk.

5. Bake in a preheated oven at 180°C/350°F/gas mark 4 for 20-30 minutes until golden brown on top.

6. Serve with salad and boiled potatoes.

🕐 15 min Preparation time
   30 min Cooking time

BROCCOLI FLAN

ingredients	Metric	Imperial	American
Shortcrust pastry (page 66)	100 g	4 oz	¼ lb
Small broccoli florets	100 g	4 oz	¼ lb
Eggs	2	2	2
Milk	150 ml	¼ pt	⅔ cup
Salt and pepper			
Cheese, grated	100 g	4 oz	1 cup

method

1. Make the pastry, roll out and use to line an 18 cm/7 in flan case.

2. Cook the broccoli in boiling water for 2 minutes then drain. Mix with the remaining ingredients and pour into the pastry case.

3. Bake in a preheated oven at 180°C/350°F/gas mark 4 for about 20-30 minutes until the filling is firm.

4. Serve hot or cold with salad.

🕐 15 min Preparation time
   30 min Cooking time

CAULIFLOWER CHEESE*

ingredients	Metric	Imperial	American
Cauliflower, cut into florets	1	1	1
Salt			
White Sauce* (page 112)	600 ml	1 pt	2 ½ cups
Pepper			
Cheddar cheese*, grated	175 g	6 oz	1 ½ cups

method

1. Cook the cauliflower in a pan of boiling salted water for 10 minutes then drain.

2. Make the white sauce, season with salt and pepper and stir in the cauliflower. Stir in most of the cheese and pour into an ovenproof dish. Sprinkle with the remaining cheese

3. Bake in a preheated oven at 200°C/400°F/gas mark 6 for 20 minutes until cooked through and golden brown.

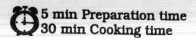
5 min Preparation time
30 min Cooking time

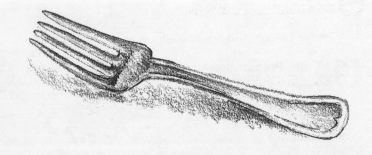

CHEESEY JACKET POTATOES*

ingredients	Metric	Imperial	American
Large potatoes	4	4	4
Butter or margarine*	60 ml	4 tbsp	4 tbsp
Cheddar cheese*, grated	100 g	4 oz	1 cup

method

1. Wash the potatoes, prick with a fork and place on a baking tray. Bake in a preheated oven at 200°C/400°F/gas mark 6 for 1-1½ hours until the potatoes are tender.

2. Slice open the potatoes and top with the butter or margarine and grated cheese.

variations

Any number of things can be used as toppings: chilli, coleslaw, curry, or leftovers from almost any of the recipes in this book. Be adventurous!

If you spike the potatoes on a potato baker or a clean 15 cm/6 in nail, they will cook more quickly.

3 min Preparation time
1-1½ hour Cooking time

69

PIZZA*

ingredients	Metric	Imperial	American
Dough:			
Plain (all-purpose) flour	225 g	8 oz	2 cups
Margarine*	50 g	2 oz	¼ cup
Water	90 ml	6 tbsp	6 tbsp
Topping:			
Can tomatoes	400 g	14 oz	14 oz
Onion, chopped	½	½	½
Tomato purée (paste)	30 ml	2 tbsp	2 tbsp
Pepper			
Vegetarian cheese*, grated	100-450 g	4 oz-1 lb	1-4 cups
Dried mixed herbs, oregano or marjoram	5 ml	1 tsp	1 tsp

method

1. Rub the flour and margarine together until the mixture looks like breadcrumbs. Add a little water at a time until the mixture makes a soft dough; you may not need all the water. Knead until smooth. Roll out to a circle on a lightly floured surface until it is as thick or thin as you prefer. Place on an oiled baking sheet.

2. Heat the topping ingredients except the cheese until most of the liquid has evaporated and the mixture is quite thick.

3. Spread the topping over the pizza base and sprinkle with as much cheese as you like. Sprinkle with the herbs. Bake in a preheated oven at 200°C/400°F/gas mark 6 for 20 minutes until browned and bubbling.

4. Serve with potato salad and garlic bread.

variations

You can use a packet pizza base mix, a ready-made pizza base or a French stick, sliced lengthways instead of making your own dough. If so, cook the pizza for a slightly shorter time.

Try different combinations of ingredients for the topping: (bell) peppers, mushrooms, olives, sweetcorn, garlic, pineapple or any thing else you fancy.

5 min Preparation time
30 min Cooking time

Side Dishes

Maybe it's me being greedy, but I do like to have lots of different things to eat at a meal. I suppose it's because you get more! Try some of these with the main meals and you'll see how much nicer it is than eating them on their own. Or serve them with hunks of crusty bread to make a main meal.

CHEESE AND MUSHROOM FRITTERS

ingredients	Metric	Imperial	American
Oil	5 ml	1 tsp	1 tsp
Mushrooms, sliced	50 g	2 oz	2 oz
Cheddar cheese, grated	175 g	3 oz	¾ cup
Batter mix (page 138)	150 ml	¼ pt	¾ cup
Oil for deep-frying			

method

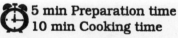

1. Heat the oil and fry the mushrooms for 2 minutes.

2. Add the mushrooms and cheese to the batter mix.

3. Heat the deep-frying oil and drop the mushrooms separately into the oil to form fritters. Cook in batches if necessary. Fry until golden. Drain well before serving.

🕐 5 min Preparation time
10 min Cooking time

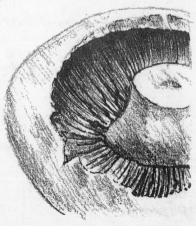

FRUITY CABBAGE*

ingredients	Metric	Imperial	American
Oil	15 ml	1 tbsp	1 tbsp
Cabbage, shredded	1	1	1
Onion, chopped	1	1	1
Garlic clove, crushed	1	1	1
Cooking (tart) apple, peeled and chopped	1	1	1
Lemon juice	10 ml	2 tsp	2 tsp
Salt and pepper			

method

1. Heat the oil and gently fry the cabbage, onion and garlic for about 5 minutes until just soft.

2. Add the apple, lemon juice, salt and pepper, cover and cook over a low heat for 10-15 minutes, stirring occasionally. Serve hot.

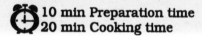
10 min Preparation time
20 min Cooking time

FRIED AUBERGINES*

ingredients	Metric	Imperial	American
Aubergines, sliced	2	2	2
Salt			
Plain (all-purpose) flour	25 g	1 oz	¼ cup
Garlic clove, crushed	1	1	1
Oil for frying			

method

1. Arrange the aubergines in a colander and sprinkle with salt. Leave to stand for 30 minutes. Rinse and drain.

2. Mix together the flour, salt and garlic. Coat the aubergines in the seasoned flour.

3. Heat the oil and fry the aubergines for a few minutes until crisp and brown on both sides.

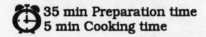 35 min Preparation time
5 min Cooking time

CREAMY PEAS*

ingredients	Metric	Imperial	American
Cooked peas	175 g	6 oz	1½ cups
White Sauce* (page 112)	300 ml	½ pt	1¼ cups
Sugar	5 ml	1 tsp	1 tsp
Salt and pepper			
Chopped fresh mint (optional)	5 ml	1 tsp	1 tsp

method

1. Add the hot peas to the sauce and seasonings.

2. Serve with nut roast or similar dishes.

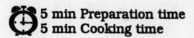 5 min Preparation time
5 min Cooking time

CAULIFLOWER FRITTERS

ingredients	Metric	Imperial	American
Small cauliflower, cut into florets	1	1	1
Salt			
Batter mix (page 138)	150 ml	¼ pt	⅔ cup
Oil for deep-frying			

method

1. Cook the cauliflower in boiling salted water for about 10 minutes until almost tender. Drain well.

2. Dip the cauliflower into the batter.

3. Heat the oil and fry the cauliflower until crisp and golden. Drain well before serving.

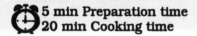 5 min Preparation time
20 min Cooking time

POTATO PUDDING

ingredients	Metric	Imperial	American
Potatoes, peeled and grated	900 g	2 lb	2 lb
Egg, beaten	1	1	1
Salt and pepper			

method

1. Mix together the potatoes, egg, salt and pepper and place in a greased ovenproof dish.

2. Bake in a preheated oven at 180°C/350°F/gas mark 4 for about 1 hour until soft in the centre and crisp on top.

3. Serve on its own or as a side dish.

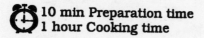
10 min Preparation time
1 hour Cooking time

POTCH*

ingredients	Metric	Imperial	American
Carrots, diced	225 g	8 oz	½ lb
Swede, diced	225 g	8 oz	½ lb
Margarine*	30 ml	2 tbsp	2 tbsp
Salt and pepper			

method

1. Cook the carrots and swede in boiling water for about 10 minutes until tender. Drain and mash with the margarine. Season to taste with salt and pepper.

2. Spoon the mixture into an ovenproof dish and bake in a preheated oven at 200°C/400°F/gas mark 6 for 10 minutes until a crust forms on the top.

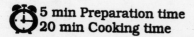
5 min Preparation time
20 min Cooking time

TANDOORI CAULIFLOWER

ingredients	Metric	Imperial	American
Small cauliflower, cut into florets	1	1	1
Water			
Tandoori spice mix	30 ml	2 tbsp	2 tbsp
Lemon juice	15 ml	1 tbsp	1 tbsp
Natural (plain) yoghurt	150 ml	¼ pt	⅓ cup

method

1. Cook the cauliflower in boiling water for 5 minutes. Drain and arrange in an ovenproof dish.

2. Mix together the remaining ingredients and pour over the cauliflower. Leave for 1 hour to marinate.

3. Cook the cauliflower in a preheated oven at 200°C/400°F/gas mark 6 for 30 minutes until soft and slightly blackened.

4. Serve with curried dishes and raita.

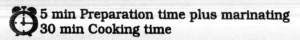

5 min Preparation time plus marinating
30 min Cooking time

CORN ON THE COB WITH BUTTER SAUCE

ingredients	Metric	Imperial	American
Corn cobs	4	4	4
Water			
Salt			
Lemon juice	30 ml	2 tbsp	2 tbsp
Sauce:			
Butter or margarine	75 g	3 oz	⅔ cup
Plain (all-purpose) flour	25 g	1 oz	2 tbsp
Milk	300 ml	½ pt	1¼ cups
Egg yolk	1	1	1
Pinch of dried basil			
Salt and pepper			

method

1. Place the corn in a saucepan and cover with water. Add a pinch of salt and the lemon juice, bring to the boil then simmer for about 20 minutes until tender. Drain and remove the leaves and strings.

2. Meanwhile, melt 25 g/1 oz/2 tbsp of the butter or margarine in a small pan. Stir in the flour then gradually whisk in the milk. Bring to the boil, whisking continuously, then lower the heat.

3. Add the egg yolk, basil, salt and pepper and the remaining butter or margarine and stir until melted. Pour the sauce over the corn.

4. Serve with French Omelette (page 46) or Vegetable Lasagne (page 53).

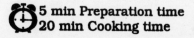 5 min Preparation time
20 min Cooking time

LEEK AND WOTSIT BAKE

ingredients	Metric	Imperial	American
Margarine	50 g	2 oz	¼ cup
Large leeks, thickly sliced	3	3	3
Plain fromage frais	250 ml	8 fl oz	1 cup
Edam cheese, grated	175 g	6 oz	1½ cups
Cheese Wotsits, crushed	30 g	1½ oz	1½ oz
Dried dill	2.5 ml	½ tsp	½ tsp

method

1. Melt the margarine and fry the leeks over a low heat for 5 minutes. Pour into an ovenproof dish.

2. Pour over the fromage frais. Sprinkle with cheese, Wotsits and dill.

3. Bake in a preheated oven at 200°C/400°F/gas mark 6 for 15 minutes until heated through.

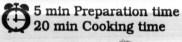
5 min Preparation time
20 min Cooking time

MUSHROOM BHAJI*

ingredients	Metric	Imperial	American
Mushrooms, sliced	175 g	6 oz	6 oz
Green (bell) pepper, sliced	1	1	1
Onion, sliced	1	1	1
Salt	2.5 ml	½ tsp	½ tsp
Curry powder	10 ml	2 tsp	2 tsp
Turmeric	5 ml	1 tsp	1 tsp
Chilli powder	1.5 ml	¼ tsp	¼ tsp
Oil	30 ml	2 tbsp	2 tbsp
Water			
Creamed coconut	25 g	1 oz	1 oz

method

1. Mix together the mushrooms, pepper, onion, salt, curry powder, turmeric and chilli powder. Stir well then leave to marinate for 10 minutes.

2. Heat the oil and fry the vegetables and spices for 10 minutes over a low heat, adding a little water and the coconut towards the end of the cooking time.

3. Serve with rice and Vegetable Curry (page 28).

⏰ 15 min Preparation time plus marinating
15 min Cooking time

BREADED MUSHROOMS

ingredients	Metric	Imperial	American
Button mushrooms	225 g	8 oz	½ lb
Eggs, beaten	2	2	2
Breadcrumbs	50 g	2 oz	½ cup
Oil for deep-frying			

method

1. Dip the mushrooms into the beaten egg and then into the breadcrumbs. Dip them again into egg then breadcrumbs.

2. Heat the oil and fry the mushrooms for 3-4 minutes until crisp and browned.

3. Serve with garlic mayonnaise.

5 min Preparation time
5 min Cooking time

STUFFED MUSHROOMS

ingredients	Metric	Imperial	American
Dry stuffing mix	100 g	4 oz	1/4 lb
Large flat mushrooms	4	4	4
Stilton cheese, grated	175 g	6 oz	1 1/2 cups

method

1. Make up the stuffing as directed on the packet.

2. Remove the mushroom stalks, chop the stalks and mix them into the stuffing. Arrange the mushroom caps in a shallow ovenproof dish, underside facing upwards. Spoon the stuffing mix into the mushroom caps and sprinkle with cheese.

3. Bake in a preheated oven at 190°C/375°F/gas mark 5 for 15-20 minutes.

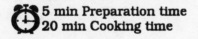 5 min Preparation time
20 min Cooking time

BUBBLE AND SQUEAK*

ingredients	Metric	Imperial	American
Mashed potato	450 g	1 lb	1 lb
Cooked Brussels sprouts or cabbage	225 g	8 oz	½ lb
Salt and pepper			
Butter or margarine* for frying			

method

1. Mix together the potato and vegetables – you can use any leftover vegetables. Season generously with salt and pepper.

2. Heat the butter or margarine. Add the vegetable mixture to the pan and press into a pancake shape. Cook until browned on the underside then turn over and brown the other side.

3. Serve on its own with ketchup, on toast, or as a side dish.

note

This is a traditional recipe for using up leftovers. Quantities are not really important just use what you have.

5 min Preparation time
15 min Cooking time

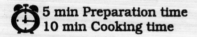

CHEESEY MASH*

ingredients	Metric	Imperial	American
Potatoes, diced	450 g	1 lb	1 lb
Salt			
Milk*	30 ml	2 tbsp	2 tbsp
Butter or margarine*	25 g	1 oz	2 tbsp
Pepper			
Cheddar cheese*, grated	50 g	2 oz	½ cup

method

1. Cook the potatoes in boiling salted water until soft. Drain.

2. Mash the potatoes with the remaining ingredients.

5 min Preparation time
10 min Cooking time

SCALLOPED SPUDS

ingredients	Metric	Imperial	American
Potatoes, sliced	450 g	1 lb	1 lb
Onion, sliced	1	1	1
Salt and pepper			
Cheddar cheese, grated	100 g	4 oz	1 cup
Egg	1	1	1
Milk	150 ml	¼ pt	⅔ cup

method

1. Grease a shallow ovenproof dish and layer the potatoes and onions in the dish, seasoning with salt and pepper as you go.

2. Mix together the cheese, egg and milk and pour over the vegetables.

3. Bake in a preheated oven at 180°C/350°F/gas mark 4 for about 1½ hours until tender throughout and browned on top.

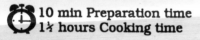 10 min Preparation time
1½ hours Cooking time

TOMATO POTATO*

ingredients	Metric	Imperial	American
Potatoes, halved	450 g	1 lb	1 lb
Salt			
Can chopped tomatoes	400 g	14 oz	14 oz
Breadcrumbs	25 g	1 oz	¼ cup
Cheddar cheese*, grated	50 g	2 oz	½ cup

method

1. Cook the potatoes in boiling salted water for about 10 minutes until just soft. Drain and arrange in an ovenproof dish.

2. Pour over the tomatoes and bake in a preheated oven at 180°C/350°F/gas mark 4 for 15 minutes.

3. Mix together the breadcrumbs and cheese and sprinkle over the top. Return to the oven or place under a hot grill (broiler) for a few minutes until the cheese is browned and bubbling.

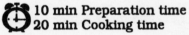 10 min Preparation time
20 min Cooking time

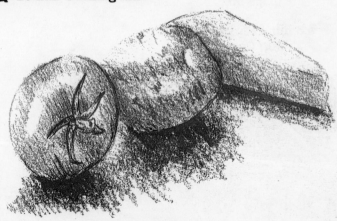

MINTY SPUDS AND PEAS*

ingredients

ingredients	Metric	Imperial	American
Oil	15 ml	1 tbsp	1 tbsp
Small onions	350 g	12 oz	¾ lb
New potatoes	675 g	1½ lb	1½ lb
Frozen peas, thawed	350 g	12 oz	3 cups
Plain (all-purpose) flour	30 ml	2 tbsp	2 tbsp
Vegetable stock	600 ml	1 pt	2½ cups
Chopped fresh mint	45 ml	3 tbsp	3 tbsp
Salt and pepper			

method

1. Heat the oil in a large pan, add the vegetables and cook for 3 minutes, stirring.

2. Sprinkle in the flour then stir in the stock, mint, salt and pepper. Bring to the boil then simmer for 20 minutes until the vegetables are tender.

3. Serve with **Vegetable Lasagne** (page 53) or **Cottage Pie** (page 50).

5 min Preparation time
25 min Cooking time

PARMESAN PASTA*

ingredients	Metric	Imperial	American
Pasta	175 g	6 oz	6 oz
Salt			
Can chopped tomatoes	400 g	14 oz	14 oz
Dried mixed herbs	5 ml	1 tsp	1 tsp
Pepper			
Margarine*	15 ml	1 tbsp	1 tbsp
Parmesan or Cheddar cheese*, grated			

method

1. Cook the pasta in boiling salted water until just tender.

2. Heat the tomatoes in a pan with the herbs and pepper.

3. Drain the pasta and return it to the hot saucepan. Toss with the margarine. Pour in the tomatoes and season to taste with salt and pepper.

4. Pour the pasta on to a serving plate and sprinkle with Parmesan cheese.

5. Serve with garlic bread as a starter or snack or with nut roast as a side dish.

5 min Preparation time
10 min Cooking time

PASTA NIÇOISE*

ingredients	Metric	Imperial	American
Pasta shapes	225 g	8 oz	½ lb
Salt			
Oil	5 ml	1 tsp	1 tsp
Garlic cloves, crushed	2	2	2
Onion, chopped	1	1	1
Tomatoes, skinned and chopped	4	4	4
Tomato purée (paste)	15 ml	1 tbsp	1 tbsp
Dried oregano	2.5 ml	½ tsp	½ tsp
Dried marjoram	2.5 ml	½ tsp	½ tsp
Pepper			

method

1. Cook the pasta in boiling salted water until just tender. Drain.

2. Meanwhile, heat the oil and fry the garlic and onion for 5 minutes. Stir in the tomatoes, tomato purée and herbs. Add the drained pasta and warm through, stirring. Season with salt and pepper.

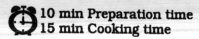

10 min Preparation time
15 min Cooking time

CHEESEY SPAGHETTI*

ingredients	Metric	Imperial	American
Spaghetti	175 g	6 oz	6 oz
Salt			
Parmesan or mature Cheddar cheese*, grated	100 g	4 oz	1 cup
Butter or margarine*	25 g	1 oz	2 tbsp
Pepper			

method

1. Cook the spaghetti in boiling salted water until just tender. Drain then return to the hot saucepan.

2. Add the cheese and butter or margarine and season with salt and pepper.

3. Serve on its own or with Swedish TVP (page 44).

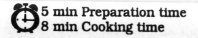 5 min Preparation time
8 min Cooking time

COURGETTE PASTA*

ingredients	Metric	Imperial	American
Margarine*	25 g	1 oz	2 tbsp
Courgettes, sliced	450 g	1 lb	1 lb
Onion, chopped	1	1	1
Pinch of dried tarragon			
Tagliatelle	225 g	8 oz	½ lb
Salt			
White Sauce* (page 112)	300 ml	½ pt	1¼ cups
Pepper			

method

1. Melt the margarine and fry the courgettes, onions and tarragon gently until soft.

2. Meanwhile, cook the tagliatelle in boiling salted water until just soft. Drain and turn into a serving dish.

3. Spoon the vegetables over the pasta. Season the white sauce with salt and pepper and pour over the dish.

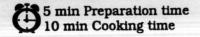

5 min Preparation time
10 min Cooking time

COUSCOUS*

ingredients	Metric	Imperial	American
Couscous	175 g	6 oz	6 oz
Oil	15 ml	1 tbsp	1 tbsp
Red or green (bell) pepper, diced	1	1	1
Onion, chopped	1	1	1
Sultanas (golden raisins)	50 g	2 oz	1/3 cup
Lemon juice	5 ml	1 tsp	1 tsp
Pinch of ground ginger			
Dash of soy sauce			
Salt and pepper			

method

1. Put the couscous into a sieve and place over a pan of water, making sure the couscous does not touch the water. Bring the water to the boil then cover and simmer for 20 minutes to steam the couscous until tender.

2. Heat the oil and fry the pepper and onion until tender. Add the couscous, sultanas and seasonings and simmer, stirring, for 2 minutes to blend the flavours.

3. Serve with spiced dishes.

⏰ 10 min Preparation time
25 min Cooking time

DHAL*

ingredients	Metric	Imperial	American
Red lentils	175 g	6 oz	1 cup
Onion, chopped	1	1	1
Garlic cloves, crushed	2	2	2
Turmeric	15 ml	1 tbsp	1 tbsp
Ground cumin	15 ml	1 tbsp	1 tbsp
Ground coriander	15 ml	1 tbsp	1 tbsp
Paprika	10 ml	2 tsp	2 tsp
Vegetable stock	600 ml	1 pt	2 ½ cups

method

1. Put all the ingredients into a saucepan and bring to the boil. Skim the top then simmer for 20-30 minutes until very mushy, stirring frequently to stop it sticking to the bottom of the pan. Add a little more water while cooking if the lentils become too dry.

2. Serve with curries as a side dish or on its own with chips.

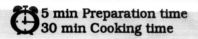
5 min Preparation time
30 min Cooking time

VEGETABLE RICE*

ingredients		Metric	Imperial	American
Long-grain rice	175 g	6 oz	¾ cup	
Vegetable stock		600 ml	1 pt	2 ½ cups
Frozen mixed vegetables, thawed		75 g	3 oz	¾ cup

method

1. Cook the rice in the stock for about 15 minutes until almost soft.

2. Add the vegetables and cook for a further 5 minutes.

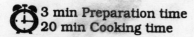
3 min Preparation time
20 min Cooking time

SPICY FRIED RICE*

ingredients	Metric	Imperial	American
Margarine*	25 g	1 oz	2 tbsp
Onion, finely chopped	1	1	1
Turmeric	5 ml	1 tsp	1 tsp
Ground cumin	5 ml	1 tsp	1 tsp
Ground coriander	5 ml	1 tsp	1 tsp
Cooked long-grain rice	175 g	6 oz	6 oz

method

1. Melt the margarine and fry the onion until soft. Add the spices and stir-fry for 2 minutes without allowing the spices to burn.

2. Stir in the rice and stir-fry for 5 minutes until hot.

3. Serve with curried or spicy dishes.

5 min Preparation time
10 min Cooking time

LEMON RICE*

ingredients	Metric	Imperial	American
Basmati or other long-grain rice	350 g	12 oz	1½ cups
Water	450 ml	¾ pt	2 cups
Garlic clove, crushed	1	1	1
Lemon grass or grated lemon rind	10 ml	2 tsp	2 tsp
Turmeric	10 ml	2 tsp	2 tsp
Creamed coconut	50 g	2 oz	2 oz
Salt and pepper			

method

1. If you are using basmati rice, soak it in boiling water for 10 minutes then rinse in cold water several times to remove the starch.

2. Place the rice, water, garlic, lemon grass or lemon rind and turmeric in a saucepan, bring to the boil then simmer for 10-20 minutes until just tender, stirring frequently.

3. Stir in the coconut and season with salt and pepper.

4. Serve with spicy dishes such as curries or chilli.

note

Lemon grass is available in supermarkets or oriental food stores. Creamed coconut is available from most supermarkets.

5 min Preparation time
20 min Cooking time

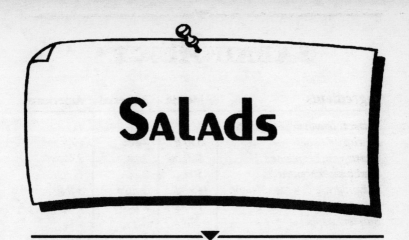

Salads

The thing with salads is that there is no real 'right' way of making them. Don't worry if you don't have some of the ingredients; replace them with something else or just forget them. It'll probably taste better that way!

SALAD ALICE*

ingredients	Metric	Imperial	American
Lettuce, leaves separated	1	1	1
Pineapple cubes	350 g	12 oz	¾ lb
Grapefruit, segmented	1	1	1
Hazelnuts, chopped	50 g	2 oz	½ cup
Olive oil	45 ml	3 tbsp	3 tbsp
Lemon juice	10 ml	2 tsp	2 tsp
Salt and pepper			

method

1. Place the lettuce leaves in a large bowl. Add the fruit and nuts.

2. Mix together the oil and lemon juice and pour over the salad. Season with salt and pepper and toss well. Chill before serving.

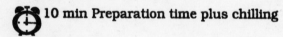 10 min Preparation time plus chilling

FROZEN CHEESE SALAD

ingredients	Metric	Imperial	American
Cottage cheese	100 g	4 oz	½ cup
Evaporated milk	100 ml	3½ fl oz	6½ tbsp
Pinch of chopped fresh chives			
Salt and pepper			

method

1. Mix all the ingredients together and press gently into a freezer container. Cover and freeze until firm.

2. Cut into slices and serve with lettuce, falafels and pitta bread.

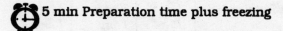 5 min Preparation time plus freezing

ORANGE AND CUCUMBER SALAD

ingredients	Metric	Imperial	American
Cottage cheese	225 g	8 oz	1 cup
Oranges, segmented	2	2	2
Cucumber, sliced	½	½	½
Oil	45 ml	3 tbsp	3 tbsp
Lemon juice	15 ml	1 tbsp	1 tbsp

method

1. Mix together all the ingredients and chill before serving.

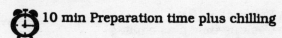 10 min Preparation time plus chilling

POTATO SALAD*

ingredients	Metric	Imperial	American
New potatoes, cut into bite-sized pieces	675 g	1½ lb	1½ lb
Hard-boiled (hard-cooked) egg, chopped (optional)	1	1	1
Chopped fresh parsley	15 ml	1 tbsp	1 tbsp
Mayonnaise*	15 ml	1 tbsp	1 tbsp
Mustard	5 ml	1 tsp	1 tsp
Wine vinegar	5 ml	1 tsp	1 tsp
Pepper			

method

1. Simmer the potatoes in boiling water for about 15 minutes until just cooked but still firm. Drain and leave to cool.

2. Mix together the remaining ingredients and add to the potatoes. Stir together well. Chill before serving.

3. This tastes better if covered and left in the fridge overnight before serving.

note

This is the best potato salad in the world! You are very fortunate that I'm sharing this with you; I should keep it all to myself.

⏰ 10 min Preparation time
15 min Cooking time plus chilling

COLESLAW*

ingredients	Metric	Imperial	American
Large carrots, grated	2	2	2
White cabbage, shredded	½	½	½
Dressing:			
Olive oil	90 ml	6 tbsp	6 tbsp
Mayonnaise*	30 ml	2 tbsp	2 tbsp
Mustard	1.5 ml	¼ tsp	¼ tsp
Pepper			

method

1. Mix together the vegetables.

2. Place all the dressing ingredients in a screw-topped jar and shake well to mix.

3. Pour the dressing over the vegetables and mix well.

variations

Mix in any other ingredients such as sultanas or grated apple to make the coleslaw more interesting.

 10 min Preparation time

RICE SALAD*

ingredients	Metric	Imperial	American
Long-grain rice	175 g	6 oz	¾ cup
Salt	2.5 ml	½ tsp	½ tsp
Turmeric	10 ml	2 tsp	2 tsp
Raisins	50 g	2 oz	⅓ cup
Banana, sliced	1	1	1
Creamed coconut, grated	50 g	2 oz	2 oz
Red (bell) pepper, diced	1	1	1
Sweetcorn	30 ml	2 tbsp	2 tbsp
Dried tarragon	2.5 ml	½ tsp	½ tsp
Few chunks of pineapple			

method

1. Cook the rice in boiling salted water with the turmeric for about 15 minutes until tender. Drain and leave to cool.

2. Mix the rice with the remaining ingredients and toss well. Chill before serving.

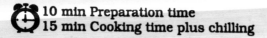
10 min Preparation time
15 min Cooking time plus chilling

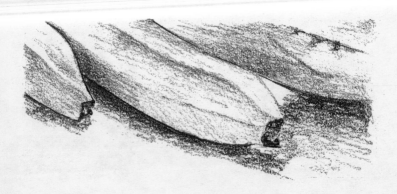

SUNSHINE RICE SALAD*

ingredients	Metric	Imperial	American
Long-grain rice	175 g	6 oz	¾ cup
Salt			
Turmeric	5 ml	1 tsp	1 tsp
Canned pineapple in juice	175 g	6 oz	6 oz
Canned sweetcorn, drained	75 g	3 oz	¾ cup
Dried tarragon	5 ml	1 tsp	1 tsp
Lemon juice	15 ml	1 tbsp	1 tbsp
Soy sauce	5 ml	1 tsp	1 tsp
Oil	15 ml	1 tbsp	1 tbsp
Salt and pepper			

method

1. Cook the rice in boiling salted water with the turmeric for about 15 minutes until tender. Drain and leave to cool.

2. Mix together all the remaining ingredients and pour over the cooled rice. Toss together well. Chill before serving.

⏰ 5 min Preparation time
15 min Cooking time plus chilling

BULGAR SALAD

ingredients	Metric	Imperial	American
Bulgar wheat	225 g	8 oz	½ lb
Bunch of spring onions, chopped	1	1	1
Eating (dessert) apples, chopped	2	2	2
Feta cheese	75 g	3 oz	¾ cup
Cashew nuts	50 g	2 oz	½ cup
Chopped fresh parsley	10 ml	2 tsp	2 tsp
Chopped fresh tarragon	10 ml	2 tsp	2 tsp
Olive oil	30 ml	2 tbsp	2 tbsp
Wine or cider vinegar	15 ml	1 tbsp	1 tbsp
Lemon juice	15 ml	1 tbsp	1 tbsp
Pepper			
Chopped fresh mint	15 ml	1 tbsp	1 tbsp
Quantity Yoghurt Dressing (page 115)	1	1	1

method

1. Soak the bulgar wheat in boiling water for 30 minutes then leave to cool.

2. Mix all the ingredients together in a large bowl then add the dressing and toss together well.

variations

You can use any dressing of your choice with this salad.

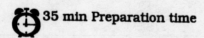 35 min Preparation time

PASTA SALAD*

ingredients	Metric	Imperial	American
Pasta shapes	100 g	4 oz	¼ lb
Salt			
Dressing:			
Garlic clove, crushed	1	1	1
Olive oil	90 ml	6 tbsp	6 tbsp
Tomato purée (paste)	5 ml	1 tsp	1 tsp
Pepper			
Pinch of dried tarragon			
Wine vinegar	5 ml	1 tsp	1 tsp

method

1. Cook the pasta in boiling salted water until just tender. Drain and leave to cool.

2. Put all the dressing ingredients into a screw-topped jar and shake well to mix. Pour over the pasta and toss together well. Chill before serving.

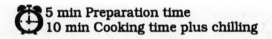

5 min Preparation time
10 min Cooking time plus chilling

EGG MAYONNAISE

ingredients	Metric	Imperial	American
Hard-boiled (hard-cooked) eggs	3	3	3
Mayonnaise	30 ml	2 tbsp	2 tbsp
Pinch of paprika or dried dill			
Salt and pepper			

method

1. Mash the eggs in a bowl. Stir in the mayonnaise, paprika or dill, salt and pepper. Chill before serving in sandwiches or on its own.

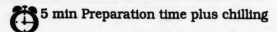 5 min Preparation time plus chilling

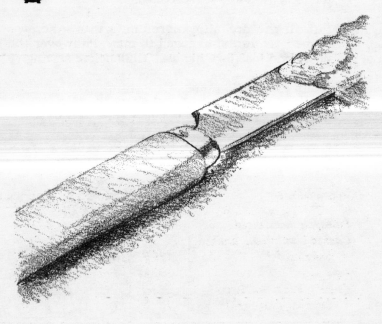

WALDORF SALAD*

ingredients	Metric	Imperial	American
Celery sticks, sliced	4	4	4
Eating (dessert) apple, diced	1	1	1
Bananas, sliced	2	2	2
Walnuts, chopped	50 g	2 oz	½ cup
Mayonnaise*	45 ml	3 tbsp	3 tbsp

method

1. Place the fruit and nuts in a large bowl and gently mix together.

2. Add the mayonnaise and toss together well. Chill before serving.

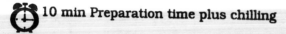 10 min Preparation time plus chilling

CHINESE BEANSPROUT SALAD*

ingredients	Metric	Imperial	American
Pineapple rings, diced	4	4	4
Canned beansprouts, drained and rinsed	175 g	6 oz	6 oz
Tofu, diced	100 g	4 oz	¼ lb
Quantity Sweet and Sour Dressing (page 119)	1	1	1

method

1. Mix together the pineapple, beansprouts and tofu. Pour over the dressing and toss well. Chill before serving.

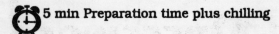 5 min Preparation time plus chilling

GRAPE AND PEAR SALAD*

ingredients

ingredients	Metric	Imperial	American
Seedless black grapes	100 g	4 oz	¼ lb
Pears, diced	2	2	2
Lancashire cheese*, cubed	100 g	4 oz	¼ lb
Grape or apple juice	45 ml	3 tbsp	3 tbsp
Dash of soy sauce			
Olive oil	15 ml	1 tbsp	1 tbsp

method

1. Mix together the fruit and cheese.

2. Mix together the juice, soy sauce and olive oil. Pour over the salad and chill before serving.

variations

You can use any crumbly cheese for this recipe.

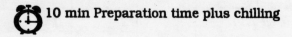 10 min Preparation time plus chilling

SAUCES, DIPS AND DRESSINGS

Use these basic, tasty sauces and dressings not just in these recipes but to spice-up plain-cooked foods such as grilled meat or microwaved fish, or to toss on your favourite salads.

SPICY TOMATO SAUCE*

ingredients	Metric	Imperial	American
Oil	15 ml	1 tbsp	1 tbsp
Onion, finely chopped	1	1	1
Can chopped tomatoes	400 g	14 oz	14 oz
Dried oregano	5 ml	1 tsp	1 tsp
Pinch of chilli powder			
Pinch of pepper			
Dash of vegetarian Worcestershire sauce			

method

1. Heat the oil and fry the onion for about 5 minutes until soft.

2. Add the remaining ingredients and simmer for 10 minutes.

3. Serve with Dolmas (page 58), pasta or Nut Roast (page 62).

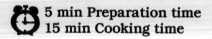
5 min Preparation time
15 min Cooking time

RAITA

ingredients	Metric	Imperial	American
Natural (plain) yoghurt	150 ml	¼ pt	⅔ cup
Chopped fresh mint	15 ml	1 tbsp	1 tbsp
Salt	1.5 ml	¼ tsp	¼ tsp
Sugar	1.5 ml	¼ tsp	¼ tsp
Cucumber, finely chopped	25 g	1 oz	1 oz
Milk	5-10 ml	1-2 tsp	1-2 tsp

method

1. Mix together all the ingredients, adding just
    enough milk to make the mixture creamy but not
    too runny. Chill before serving.

2. Serve with curried dishes to cool the mouth.

note

It has taken me years to work out how to make
this the same as in my local Indian restaurant.
This is the closest I have got so far.

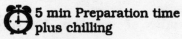

🕐 5 min Preparation time
plus chilling

WHITE SAUCE*

ingredients	Metric	Imperial	American
Margarine*	25 g	1 oz	2 tbsp
Plain (all-purpose) flour	25 g	1 oz	¼ cup
Milk*	300 ml	½ pt	1¼ cups
Salt and pepper			

method

1. Melt the margarine in a saucepan over a medium heat.

2. Stir in the flour over a gentle heat and cook for about 1 minute, stirring continuously.

3. Remove from the heat and gradually stir in the milk until smooth.

4. Return to the heat and whisk while bringing to the boil. The sauce will thicken. Lower the heat and keep whisking until thick and smooth.

note

This is used in a number of recipes and is very handy as a base sauce.

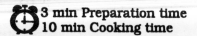
3 min Preparation time
10 min Cooking time

COCKTAIL SAUCE*

ingredients	Metric	Imperial	American
Mayonnaise*	60 ml	4 tbsp	4 tbsp
Tomato ketchup (catsup)	30 ml	2 tbsp	2 tbsp

method

1. Mix together the mayonnaise and ketchup and chill well before serving.

2. Serve with raw vegetable sticks, as a dip or salad dressing.

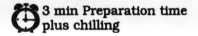 3 min Preparation time
plus chilling

GARLIC MAYONNAISE DIP*

ingredients	Metric	Imperial	American
Garlic clove, crushed	1	1	1
Mayonnaise*	45 ml	3 tbsp	3 tbsp
Pinch of pepper			

method

1. Mix together all the ingredients and chill before serving.

note

This is great for dipping vegetables into, especially deep-fried mushrooms.

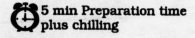 5 min Preparation time
plus chilling

GINGER DIP*

ingredients	Metric	Imperial	American
Oil	90 ml	6 tbsp	6 tbsp
Soy sauce	15 ml	1 tbsp	1 tbsp
Lemon juice	15 ml	1 tbsp	1 tbsp
Garlic clove, crushed	1	1	1
Chopped fresh ginger	2.5 ml	½ tsp	½ tsp

method

1. Mix together all the ingredients well.

note

This is great for dipping vegetables into, especially deep-fried mushrooms.

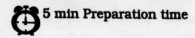 5 min Preparation time

KIDNEY BEAN PÂTÉ*

ingredients	Metric	Imperial	American
Quantity Squashed Kidney Beans (page 35), omitting the cheese			

method

1. Make the beans as directed on page 35, omitting the cheese. Allow to cool.

2. Mash the beans well with a fork then press into a pâté dish. Chill.

3. Serve with toast.

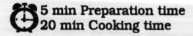
5 min Preparation time
20 min Cooking time

YOGHURT DRESSING

ingredients	Metric	Imperial	American
Natural (plain) yoghurt	150 ml	¼ pt	⅔ cup
Soft blue cheese	15 ml	1 tbsp	1 tbsp
Chopped fresh dill	5 ml	1 tsp	1 tsp

method

1. Mix together all the ingredients and chill before serving.

5 min Preparation time
plus chilling

VINAIGRETTE DRESSING*

ingredients	Metric	Imperial	American
White wine vinegar	45 ml	1 tbsp	1 tbsp
Olive oil	90 ml	6 tbsp	6 tbsp
Pepper			
Chopped fresh chives	15 ml	1 tbsp	1 tbsp
Dash of lemon juice			

method

1. Mix together all the ingredients and chill before serving.

 5 min Preparation time plus chilling

PEANUT DRESSING*

ingredients	Metric	Imperial	American
Peanut butter	60 ml	4 tbsp	4 tbsp
Olive oil	30 ml	2 tbsp	2 tbsp
Lemon juice	5 ml	1 tsp	1 tsp
Soy sauce	5 ml	1 tsp	1 tsp
Pinch of dried tarragon			

method

1. Mix together all the ingredients and chill before serving.

2. Serve as a dip or salad dressing.

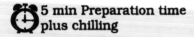 5 min Preparation time
plus chilling

HOT YOGHURT DIP

ingredients	Metric	Imperial	American
Natural (plain) yoghurt	60 ml	4 tbsp	4 tbsp
Pinch of chilli powder			
Pinch of salt			
Pinch of sugar			

method

1. Mix together all the ingredients and chill before serving.

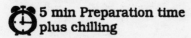 5 min Preparation time
plus chilling

CURRIED MAYONNAISE*

ingredients	Metric	Imperial	American
Mayonnaise*	60 ml	4 tbsp	4 tbsp
Garlic clove, crushed	1	1	1
Curry powder	2.5 ml	½ tsp	½ tsp
Lemon juice	2.5 ml	½ tsp	½ tsp

method

1. Mix together all the ingredients and chill before serving.

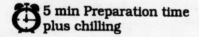 5 min Preparation time
plus chilling

SWEET AND SOUR DRESSING*

ingredients	Metric	Imperial	American
Pineapple juice	120 ml	4 fl oz	½ cup
Soy sauce	5 ml	1 tsp	1 tsp
Tomato purée (paste)	2.5 ml	½ tsp	½ tsp
Pepper			

method

1. Mix together all the ingredients and chill before serving.

2. Use as a dressing for salad such as Chinese Beansprout Salad (page 107).

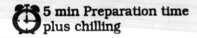 5 min Preparation time
plus chilling

SNACKS

Here are a few things you might like to try late at night for a snack or if your mum comes to visit – she'll be well impressed that you can bake scones (mothers love scones!).

CHEESEY BREAD*

ingredients	Metric	Imperial	American
Small uncut loaf	1	1	1
Edam or hard cheese*, sliced	225 g	8 oz	½ lb
Sweet pickle			

method

1. Cut the loaf into slices but don't cut right through so that each slice is still attached at the bottom.

2. Put a slice of cheese and a spoon of pickle between each slice. Wrap the loaf in foil.

3. Bake in a preheated oven at 220°C/425°F/gas mark 7 for 15-20 minutes.

variation

Try other cheeses such as Brie or Cheddar. Also, you can add tomatoes or fruit to the cheese.

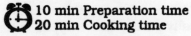 10 min Preparation time
20 min Cooking time

GARLIC BREAD*

ingredients	Metric	Imperial	American
Garlic cloves, crushed	2	2	2
Margarine*	150 g	5 oz	⅔ cup
Chopped fresh parsley	15 ml	1 tbsp	1 tbsp
French stick	1	1	1

method

1. Mix together the garlic, margarine and parsley.

2. Cut the bread into 5 cm/2 in slices without cutting right through at the bottom.

3. Spread each side of the slices with the garlic butter. Wrap the loaf in foil and bake in a preheated oven at 200°C/400°F/gas mark 6 for 20 minutes.

4. Serve as a snack or with salads or pizza.

note

This is gorgeous; really garlicy and dripping with marg.

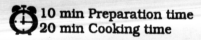 10 min Preparation time
20 min Cooking time

BANANA TEA BREAD

ingredients	Metric	Imperial	American
Margarine	100 g	4 oz	½ cup
Brown sugar	100 g	4 oz	½ cup
Bananas, mashed	3	3	3
Egg	1	1	1
Honey	15 ml	1 tbsp	1 tbsp
Cinnamon	1.5 ml	¼ tsp	¼ tsp
Self-raising (self-rising) flour	225 g	8 oz	2 cups
Baking powder	5 ml	1 tsp	1 tsp
Milk	45 ml	3 tbsp	3 tbsp

method

1. Soften the margarine then mix in the sugar until smooth.

2. Add the bananas, egg, honey and cinnamon.

3. Slowly mix in the flour and baking powder, stirring it well in. Stir in the milk.

4. Spoon into a greased loaf tin and bake in a preheated oven at 160°C/325°F/gas mark 3 for 1-1½ hours until firm.

15 min Preparation time
1-1½ hours Cooking time

HASH BROWNS*

ingredients	Metric	Imperial	American
Oil	45 ml	3 tbsp	3 tbsp
Onion, chopped	1	1	1
Potatoes, finely diced	450 g	1 lb	1 lb
Salt and pepper			

method

1. Heat the oil and fry the onion over a low heat for 5 minutes until soft. Transfer to a plate.

2. Add the potatoes to the pan and fry for 10-15 minutes until golden on the outside and soft on the inside.

3. Return the onions to the pan and season well with salt and pepper. Cook until warmed through.

4. Serve with fried eggs.

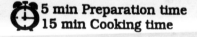 5 min Preparation time
15 min Cooking time

POTATO CRISPS*

ingredients	Metric	Imperial	American
Salt			
Clean potato peelings			

method

1. Pour a thin layer of salt on to a baking tray.
   Spread the potato peelings over the top and bake
   in a preheated oven at 200°C/400°F/gas mark 6
   for about 20 minutes until crispy.

note

This is ideal if you have the oven on for something
else; the temperature is not critical. It is also a
very efficient way of using up all the leftover potato
peelings!

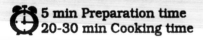 5 min Preparation time
20-30 min Cooking time

EGGY BREAD

ingredients	Metric	Imperial	American
Eggs	4	4	4
Dash of milk			
Salt and pepper			
Slices bread	6	6	6
Oil for frying			

method

1. Break the eggs into a bowl and beat with the milk and salt and pepper.

2. Cut each slice of bread into quarters and dip into the egg mixture until completely coated.

3. Heat the oil and fry the soaked bread until browned on both sides. Sprinkle with salt and serve hot.

note

The perfect late night snack!

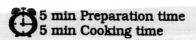
5 min Preparation time
5 min Cooking time

POTATO CAKES*

ingredients	Metric	Imperial	American
Oil	5 ml	1 tsp	1 tsp
Onion, chopped	1	1	1
Cold mashed potatoes	225 g	8 oz	½ lb
Dried mixed herbs	15 ml	1 tbsp	1 tbsp
Cheddar cheese*, grated	50 g	2 oz	½ cup
Salt and pepper			
Paprika	5 ml	1 tsp	1 tsp
Plain (all-purpose) flour	50 g	2 oz	½ cup
Oil for frying			

method

1. Heat the oil and fry the onion over a low heat for 5 minutes.

2. Mix together the onions, potatoes, herbs, cheese, salt, pepper and paprika. Shape the mixture into burger shapes and dust with flour.

3. Heat the oil and fry the cakes for about 10 minutes until browned on both sides.

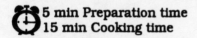
5 min Preparation time
15 min Cooking time

CHEESE PÂTÉ

ingredients	Metric	Imperial	American
Cheddar cheese, grated	100 g	4 oz	1 cup
Mature Stilton cheese, grated	100 g	4 oz	1 cup
Margarine	25 g	1 oz	2 tbsp
White wine or stock	45 ml	3 tbsp	3 tbsp
Salt and pepper			

method

1. Mix all the ingredients together to make a smooth paste. Press into a dish and cover with foil. Chill before serving.

2. Serve as a starter or snack with warm toast or crackers.

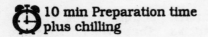 10 min Preparation time plus chilling

128

CHEESE CRUNCHIES

ingredients	Metric	Imperial	American
Slices bread	8	8	8
Margarine			
Marmite			
Cream cheese	100 g	4 oz	½ cup
Cornflakes, crushed	50 g	2 oz	2 oz

method

1. Make the bread, margarine and marmite into sandwiches then cut them into 2.5 cm/1 in cubes.

2. Spread each cube with cream cheese on all sides then toss in the cornflakes. Serve.

⏰ 10 min Preparation time

SCONES*

ingredients	Metric	Imperial	American
Self-raising (self-rising) flour	450 g	1 lb	4 cups
Baking powder	30 ml	2 tbsp	2 tbsp
Margarine*	75 g	3 oz	1/3 cup
Milk*	300 ml	1/2 pt	1 1/4 cups

method

1. Mix the flour and baking powder. Rub in the margarine until the mixture resembles breadcrumbs.

2. Gradually add the milk until the mixture forms a dough. Roll out on a floured surface to about 2.5 cm/1 in thick. Cut into circles with a biscuit (cookie) cutter.

3. Place on a greased baking tray and bake in a preheated oven at 220°C/425°F/gas mark 7 for about 12 minutes until well risen and golden brown.

variations

You can add cherries, grated cheese, raisins, sultanas (golden raisins) or honey to the mixture before baking. If you add honey, add a little more flour to maintain the consistency

5 min Preparation time
15 min Cooking time

Puddings and Sweet Things

Puds my favourite! Here are lots of easy, sticky puds to make and all of them outrageously fattening. Pig out!

BLACKBERRY CRUMBLE*

ingredients	Metric	Imperial	American
Cooking (tart) apples, peeled and chopped	450 g	1 lb	1 lb
Sugar	15 ml	1 tbsp	1 tbsp
Water	45 ml	3 tbsp	3 tbsp
Blackberries	175 g	6 oz	6 oz
Crumble:			
Plain (all-purpose) flour	100 g	4 oz	1 cup
Pinch of salt			
Margarine*	50 g	2 oz	¼ cup
Brown sugar	50 g	2 oz	¼ cup
Cinnamon	2.5 ml	½ tsp	½ tsp

method

1. Put the apples into a saucepan with the sugar and water. Heat gently, stirring occasionally, until the apples have gone mushy. Remove from the heat and stir in the blackberries. Pour into an ovenproof dish.

2. Mix the flour and salt then rub in the margarine until the mixture looks like crumbs. Stir in the sugar and cinnamon. Sprinkle over the fruit.

3. Bake in a preheated oven at 190°C/375°F/gas mark 5 for 20 minutes.

4. Serve with custard.

10 min Preparation time
20 min Cooking time

RICE PUDDING*

ingredients	Metric	Imperial	American
Short-grain rice	100 g	4 oz	½ cup
Milk*	1.2 l	2 pts	5 cups
Sugar	50 g	2 oz	¼ cup
Pinch of grated nutmeg			
Margarine*	15 ml	1 tbsp	1 tbsp

method

1. Put the rice and half the milk into a saucepan, bring to the boil then simmer for 20-25 minutes until the milk is nearly all absorbed.

2. Add all the remaining ingredients except the margarine then pour into a greased ovenproof dish. Dot with margarine.

3. Bake in a preheated oven at 150°C/300°F/gas mark 2 for about 1½ hours.

4. Serve hot or cold.

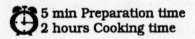 5 min Preparation time
2 hours Cooking time

DRUNKEN PEARS*

ingredients	Metric	Imperial	American
Brown sugar	15 ml	1 tbsp	1 tbsp
Lemon juice	5 ml	1 tsp	1 tsp
Red wine	300 ml	½ pt	1¼ cups
Pears, peeled	4	4	4

method

1. Dissolve the sugar and lemon juice in the wine over a gentle heat.

2. Cut a slice off the bottom of the pears so that they stand upright and remove the core from the base. Stand them in a dish and pour over the wine. Cover with foil or a lid.

3. Bake in a preheated oven at 160°C/325°F/gas mark 3 for 30 minutes.

note

Prepare the pears immediately before cooking so that thay don't discolour

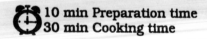

10 min Preparation time
30 min Cooking time

APPLE MUESLI*

ingredients	Metric	Imperial	American
Cooking (tart) apples, peeled and chopped	2	2	2
Blackberries	225 g	8 oz	½ lb
Lemon juice	15 ml	1 tbsp	1 tbsp
Brown sugar (optional)	15 ml	1 tbsp	1 tbsp
Muesli	150 g	5 oz	5 oz

method

1. Simmer the fruit in the lemon juice and a little water until soft. Add the sugar, if using; if you prefer a sharper taste, leave it out. Place in a flameproof dish and cover with muesli. Sprinkle a little sugar on top, if liked.

2. Place under a low grill (broiler) for 10 minutes until the muesli is golden.

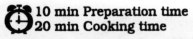
10 min Preparation time
20 min Cooking time

BAKED APPLES*

ingredients	Metric	Imperial	American
Cooking (tart) apples	4	4	4
Strawberry jam			
Brown sugar			
Water			

method

1. Remove the cores from the apples and cut a line around the centre of the apples. Stand them in an ovenproof dish.

2. Fill the holes with jam and sprinkle with a little sugar. Add about 2.5 cm/1 in of water to the bottom of the dish.

3. Bake in a preheated oven at 180°C/350°F/gas mark 4 for about 1 hour.

4. Serve hot with custard.

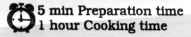 5 min Preparation time
1 hour Cooking time

CHOCOLATE BANANAS

ingredients	Metric	Imperial	American
Bananas, unpeeled	4	4	4
Chocolate squares	4	4	4

method

1. Make a slit in the skin along each banana. Poke a chunk of chocolate into the hole and close the skin around it.

2. Bake in a preheated oven at 200°C/400°F/gas mark 6 for 10 minutes until the chocolate has just started to melt.

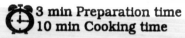 3 min Preparation time
10 min Cooking time

PINEAPPLE FRITTERS*

ingredients	Metric	Imperial	American
Batter:			
Plain (all-purpose) flour	225 g	8 oz	2 cups
Baking powder	5 ml	1 tsp	1 tsp
Pinch of salt			
*Water or milk**	300 ml	½ pt	1¼ cups
Fruit:			
16 pineapple rings			
Plain (all-purpose) flour			
Oil for frying			

method

1. Put the dry batter ingredients into a bowl and make a well in the centre. Gradually pour in the liquid, whisking to make a smooth paste.

2. Dip the pineapple rings in flour then in the batter.

3. Heat the oil and fry the fritters in hot oil until crispy.

4. Serve hot with maple syrup or ice cream.

variations

You can use the batter with any combination of hard fruits such as eating (dessert) apples or pears.

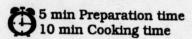 5 min Preparation time
10 min Cooking time

HONEY BREAD PUDDING

ingredients	Metric	Imperial	American
Slices bread, crusts removed	8	8	8
Margarine	25 g	1 oz	2 tbsp
Honey	45 ml	3 tbsp	3 tbsp
Eggs	3	3	3
Milk	450 ml	¾ pt	2 cups
Sugar	15 ml	1 tbsp	1 tbsp

method

1. Spread the bread with margarine and honey, cut in halves and layer in an ovenproof dish.

2. Mix together the eggs, milk and sugar and pour over the bread.

3. Bake in a preheated oven at 180°C/350°F/gas mark 4 for about 40 minutes until firm.

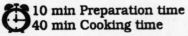 10 min Preparation time
40 min Cooking time

GRILLED GRAPEFRUIT*

ingredients	Metric	Imperial	American
Grapefruits, halved	2	2	2
Brown sugar	60 ml	4 tbsp	4 tbsp

method

1. Sprinkle each grapefruit half with sugar. Place under a hot grill (broiler) for 3 minutes until the sugar has gone sticky.

note

This is traditionally served as a starter, but it makes a nice pud, too. It is easier to eat if you cut down next to each membrane before cooking to release the segments of fruit.

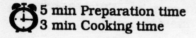

5 min Preparation time
3 min Cooking time

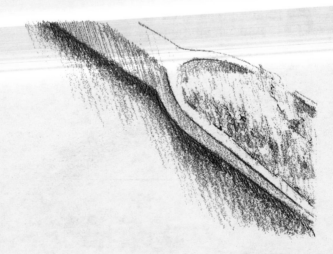

FRUIT YOGHURT

ingredients	Metric	Imperial	American
Natural (plain) yoghurt	300 ml	½ pt	1¼ cups
Can fruit	400 g	14 oz	14 oz

method

1. Drain the fruit, reserving the juice. Add the fruit to the yoghurt with enough juice to make it the consistency you prefer. Chill before serving.

note

This tastes quite different from shop-bought yoghurt. You may want to sweeten it with a little sugar or honey, or use fruit with syrup rather than natural juice.

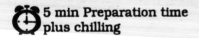
5 min Preparation time
plus chilling

BANANA FLAN

ingredients	Metric	Imperial	American
Raspberry jam			
Sponge flan case	1	1	1
Bananas, sliced	3-4	3-4	3-4
Lemon juice	15 ml	1 tbsp	1 tbsp
Whipping cream, whipped*	250 ml	8 fl oz	1 cup

method

1. Spread the jam over the flan case then arrange the bananas on top, squashing them gently.

2. Sprinkle with lemon juice to taste, cover with cream and chill before serving.

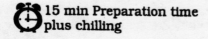 15 min Preparation time
plus chilling

SOFT FRUIT CHEESE

ingredients	Metric	Imperial	American
Soft fruit such as strawberries or raspberries	225 g	8 oz	½ lb
Low fat soft cheese	225 g	8 oz	½ lb
Sugar	15 ml	1 tbsp	1 tbsp
Lemon juice	5 ml	1 tsp	1 tsp

method

1. Squash the berries then stir in the remaining ingredients. Mix with a fork until fairly smooth. Chill before serving.

note

You can use canned fruit if the fruit is not in season; a little expensive, but nice for a change.

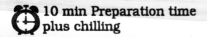 10 min Preparation time
plus chilling

APA JELLY

ingredients	Metric	Imperial	American
Packet vegetarian raspberry jelly	600 ml	1 pt	2 ½ cups
Evaporated milk	200 ml	7 fl oz	1 cup scant

method

1. Make up the jelly as directed on the packet but use 200 ml/7fl oz/scant 1 cup less water. Leave for 12 hours in the fridge until only just set.

2. Pour in the evaporated milk and whisk in with a fork. Leave to set in the fridge.

note

My friend Kate and I used to eat this all the time when we lived in London and had no money at all. You can use any flavour jelly you like, but we found raspberry tasted the best.

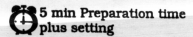 5 min Preparation time plus setting

QUARK DESSERT

ingredients	Metric	Imperial	American
Packet vegetarian jelly	600 ml	1 pt	2½ cups
Quark	100 g	4 oz	¼ lb

method

1. Make up the jelly and chill until just set.

2. Whisk in the quark and chill until set.

10 min Preparation time
plus setting

QUICK TRIFLE

ingredients	Metric	Imperial	American
Swiss roll, sliced	1	1	1
Can peach slices	200 g	7 oz	7 oz
Packet vegetarian raspberry jelly	1	1	1
Packet Peach Dessert Whip, made up	1	1	1

method

1. Arrange Swiss roll slices in the bottom of a dish. Drain the peaches, reserving the juice, and spoon the fruit over the Swiss roll.

2. Make up the jelly, using the fruit juice instead of some of the water. Pour over the sponge and fruit and leave for a few hours until set.

3. Spoon over the dessert whip 1 hour before serving.

⏰ 10 min Preparation time
plus setting

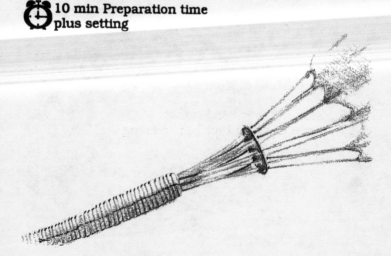

SUMMER PUDDING*

ingredients	Metric	Imperial	American
Soft fruit such as raspberries, blackberries and blackcurrants	900 g	2 lb	2 lb
Brown sugar	100-175 g	4-6 oz	½-¾ cup
Pinch of cinnamon			
Slices white bread, crusts removed	8	8	8

method

1. Cook the fruit, sugar and cinnamon until the fruit is just soft, adding the quantity of sugar appropriate to the fruit you are using.

2. Cutting the bread if necessary, line a large bowl with the bread, covering the bottom and sides and reserving a slice for the top.

3. Pour in the fruit and cover with the reserved bread. Press down lightly with a small plate and weigh down with a can. Chill overnight.

4. It is ready to eat when the fruit juice has soaked through the bread. Turn out of the bowl and serve with custard or ice cream.

10 min Preparation time
15 min Cooking time plus chilling

GINGER RHUBARB CRISP*

ingredients	Metric	Imperial	American
Rhubarb, chopped into small pieces	225 g	8 oz	½ lb
Brown sugar	25 g	1 oz	2 tbsp
Plain (all-purpose) flour	25 g	1 oz	¼ cup
Water	15 ml	1 tbsp	1 tbsp
Margarine*	25 g	1 oz	2 tbsp
Ginger biscuits, crushed	6	6	6
Double or clotted cream* to serve			
Brown sugar for sprinkling			

method

1. Cook the rhubarb in a saucepan with the sugar, flour, water and margarine for about 10 minutes until mushy.

2. Press the crushed biscuits into the bottom of a dish or serving bowls. Chill.

3. Pour the rhubarb on to the biscuits and finish with the cream and a little sugar. Chill well before serving.

⏰ 15 min Preparation time plus chilling

CARROT CAKE*

ingredients	Metric	Imperial	American
Self-raising (self-rising) flour	225 g	8 oz	2 cups
Baking powder	15 ml	1 tbsp	1 tbsp
Margarine*	150 g	5 oz	⅔ cup
Brown sugar	100 g	4 oz	½ cup
Large carrots, grated	2	2	2

method

1. Mix the flour and baking powder.

2. Melt the margarine and sugar then pour into the flour and mix well. Stir in the carrots. Pour into a greased loaf tin.

3. Bake in a preheated oven at 160°C/325°F/gas mark 3 for 1 hour until a knife inserted into the centre of the cake comes out clean.

note

This is the most moist, delicious cake there ever was, and it doesn't taste a bit healthy!

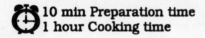 10 min Preparation time
1 hour Cooking time

PINEAPPLE LOAF

ingredients	Metric	Imperial	American
Plain (all-purpose) flour	350 g	12 oz	3 cups
Baking powder	15 ml	1 tbsp	1 tbsp
Bicarbonate of soda (baking soda)	2.5 ml	½ tsp	½ tsp
Light brown sugar	100 g	4 oz	½ cup
Margarine	150 g	5 oz	⅔ cup
Eggs, beaten	3	3	3
Milk	30 ml	2 tbsp	2 tbsp
Cinnamon	5 ml	1 tsp	1 tsp
Honey	30 ml	2 tbsp	2 tbsp
Pineapple rings with juice, cut into chunks	4	4	4

method

1. Mix all the ingredients together then pour into a greased loaf tin.

2. Bake on a low shelf in a preheated oven at 180°C/350°F/gas mark 4 for about 1 hour until firm.

3. Serve warm or cold.

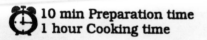
10 min Preparation time
1 hour Cooking time

CLOTTED CREAM BUNS

ingredients	Metric	Imperial	American
Clotted cream	100 ml	3 fl oz	6½ tbsp
Self-raising (self-rising) flour	225 g	8 oz	2 cups
Egg	1	1	1
Sugar	100 g	4 oz	½ cup
Milk	45-60 ml	3-4 tbsp	3-4 tbsp

method

1. Mix the cream and flour together. Add the remaining ingredients and mix to a soft dough. Shape into about 12 flattened circles and place on a greased baking tray.

2. Bake in a preheated oven at 220°C/425°F/gas mark 7 for 10-15 minutes.

note

These are really tasty on their own or with jam and more cream; not for the weight conscious.

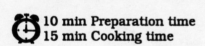
10 min Preparation time
15 min Cooking time

FLAPJACKS*

ingredients	Metric	Imperial	American
Margarine*	100 g	4 oz	½ cup
Brown sugar	75 g	3 oz	⅓ cup
Golden (corn) syrup	60 ml	4 tbsp	4 tbsp
Rolled oats	300 g	10 oz	10 oz

method

1. Melt the margarine, sugar and syrup in a saucepan over a low heat.

2. Stir in the oats until totally covered. Spoon into a greased baking tray and spread until about 1cm/ ¼ in thick.

3. Bake in a preheated oven at 180°C/350°F/gas mark 4 for about 25 minutes until golden. Leave to cool in the tray then cut into squares.

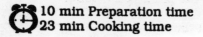
10 min Preparation time
23 min Cooking time

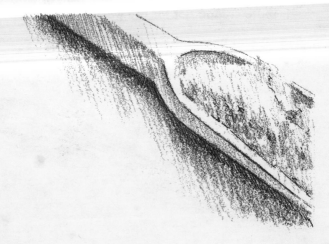

CHOCOLATE SQUIDGE

ingredients	Metric	Imperial	American
Condensed milk	60 ml	4 tbsp	4 tbsp
Drinking chocolate	60 ml	4 tbsp	4 tbsp
Margarine, melted	50 g	2 oz	¼ cup
Icing sugar	225 g	8 oz	1 cup

method

1. Mix together the milk, drinking chocolate and margarine.

2. Gradually add the icing sugar until you have a lump of squidgy brown stuff that will absorb no more sugar. Flatten to about 1 cm/½ in thick and cut into squares. Chill for a few hours.

note

This is incredibly sweet. You will lose your teeth, if you have any after the pineapple fritters.

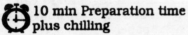 10 min Preparation time plus chilling

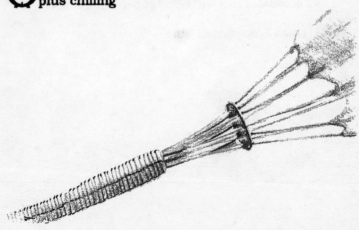

CORNFLAKE CAKES*

ingredients	Metric	Imperial	American
Margarine*	75 g	3 oz	1/3 cup
Golden (corn) syrup	75 ml	5 tbsp	5 tbsp
Drinking chocolate	100 g	4 oz	1/4 lb
OR Cocoa	45 ml	3 tbsp	3 tbsp
Cornflakes	100-175 g	4-6 oz	4-6 oz

method

1. Melt the margarine and syrup in a pan. Stir in the chocolate or cocoa.

2. Gradually stir in enough cornflakes so that they are coated in the mxiture.

3. Put spoonfuls into paper cases and leave to cool or eat hot if you can't wait.

note

I sometimes make these late at night and I can eat five or six before my teeth start to hurt from all the sweetness! You will need paper cake cases.

 10 min Preparation time

CHOCOLATE BAR COOKIES

ingredients	Metric	Imperial	American
Margarine	50 g	2 oz	¼ cup
Caster sugar	50 g	2 oz	¼ cup
Egg	1	1	1
Self-raising (self-rising) flour	175 g	6 oz	1½ cups
Vegetarian caramel carob bars, chopped	2	2	2

method

1. Melt the margarine in a saucepan. Stir in the sugar then leave to cool slightly.

2. Add the egg, flour and carob bars and mix to a lumpy dough. Make into about 20 small flat circles about 4 cm/1½ in across and place on a greased baking sheet.

3. Bake in a preheated oven at 190°C/375°F/gas mark 5 for 15-20 minutes.

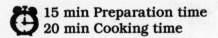 15 min Preparation time
20 min Cooking time

SHORTBREAD BISCUITS*

ingredients	Metric	Imperial	American
Self-raising (self-rising) flour	175 g	6 oz	1½ cups
Pinch of salt			
Margarine*	100 g	4 oz	½ cup
Caster sugar	50 g	2 oz	¼ cup

method

1. Mix the flour and salt. Rub in the margarine then the sugar and mix to a thick dough.

2. Roll out into a circle or square on a floured surface to 1 cm/½ in thick. Place on a greased baking tray and mark into wedges or biscuit shapes with a knife.

3. Bake in a preheated oven at 220°C/425°F/gas mark 7 for 15-20 minutes until golden. Leave to cool on the tray.

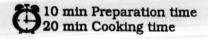 10 min Preparation time
20 min Cooking time

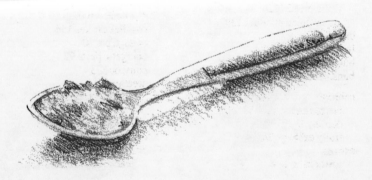

INDEX